DAY OF TEARS

Awards and Praise for *Day of Tears*

2006 Coretta Scott King Author Award Winner

A 2006 ALA Notable Children's Book

A 2006 YALSA Best Book for Young Adults

A 2006 Bank Street Best Children's Book of the Year

VOYA Top Shelf Fiction For Middle Grade Readers

Booklist Editor's Choice, 2005

Booklist Top Ten Historical Fiction for Youth, 2005

Booklist Top Ten Black History, 2006

Chicago Public Library Best of the Best, 2005

New York Public Library 100 Books for Reading and Sharing, 2005

New York Public Library Books for the Teen Age, 2006

A NCTE 2006 Notable Children's Book in the Language Arts

A *Disney Adventures* Best Historical Fiction Book of 2005

Cooperative Children's Book Center Choices, 2006

The Boston Authors Club Julia Ward Howe Young Readers Award, Finalist

Georgia Peach Book Award for Teen Readers, Finalist

DAY OF TEARS

a novel in dialogue

JULIUS LESTER

Disney • JUMP AT THE SUN
LOS ANGELES NEW YORK

For my grandson,
Theodore Morton Lester

Text copyright © 2005 by Julius Lester

For information address Disney• Jump at the Sun,
125 West End Avenue, New York, New York 10023.

Printed in the United States of America
First Disney• Jump at the Sun Hardcover Edition, April 2005
First Disney• Jump at the Sun Paperback Edition, April 2007
13
Text set in Baskerville
Text design by Angela Corbo Gier

Library of Congress Control Number for the Hardcover Edition:
2005298043
ISBN-13: 978-1-4231-0409-4
ISBN-10: 1-4231-0409-9

Visit www.DisneyBooks.com
FAC-025438-15336

SUSTAINABLE
FORESTRY
INITIATIVE
Certified Chain of Custody
Promoting Sustainable Forestry
www.sfiprogram.org
SFI-01054
The SFI label applies to the text stock

PRINCIPAL CHARACTERS

❧ SLAVES ON MASTER BUTLER'S PLANTATION ❧

EMMA
She is twelve when the story begins

GEORGE
Runaway

JOE

MATTIE
Cook and housekeeper.
Wife of Will, mother of Emma

REBECCA
Runaway

WILL
Master Butler's manservant.
Husband of Mattie, father of Emma

❧ SLAVES ON MISTRESS HENFIELD'S PLANTATION ❧

CHARLES
Son of Sampson, husband of Winnie

SAMPSON
Father of Charles

WINNIE
Wife of Charles

❧ THE BUTLER FAMILY ❧

FANNY KEMBLE
*English actress; former wife of Pierce Butler,
mother of Sarah and Frances Butler*

FRANCES BUTLER
Pierce Butler's younger daughter

PIERCE BUTLER
*Owner of the plantation.
Father of Sarah and Frances*

SARAH BUTLER
Pierce Butler's older daughter

❧ THE HENFIELD FAMILY ❧

MISTRESS HENFIELD
Owner of Henfield plantation

❧ SLAVE OWNERS AND BUSINESSMEN ❧

RODNEY DENMAN
Slave owner at auction

JEREMIAH HENRY
Abolitionist and store owner in northern Kentucky

JENKINS
Overseer on the Butler plantation

JAKE PENDLE
Kentucky slave owner.
Neighbor of Mistress Henfield

SAM ELLINGTON
Slave owner at auction

GEORGE WEEMS
Slave auctioneer

❧ LATER GENERATIONS ❧

JESSIE MAE
Emma's granddaughter

SARAH
Emma's oldest daughter

DAY OF TEARS

1

The Kitchen

mattie

It's been three days since we've seen the sun. Yesterday it started raining and it hasn't stopped since. The rain is coming down as hard as regret. Will said the rain started up just when the selling began. I ain't never seen a rain like this. Will said, "This ain't rain. This is God's tears."

will

Soon as the slave-seller called the name of the first slave he was going to put up for sale, the gray clouds turned black as a burned log. Lightning so bright flashed across the face of heaven, my eyes trembled in their sockets. Thunder rolled from one side of the sky to the other, back and forth, back and forth. My heart was jumping like it wanted to run out of my body and find some place to hide. Then down came the rain, hard as sorrow.

mattie

Every morning since I can remember, I done stood here in this kitchen. When I was a girl it was my mama what stood at this stove fixing breakfast for the master and his family. That was back in the time of Master Butler's father, Ransome. He would rise up out of his grave if he knew Master Pierce had lost so much money playing cards that he's selling off practically all his slaves to pay what he owe.

will

White folks have come from all over. Yesterday they was buying up slaves as quick as the slave-seller could get 'em up on the block. Some of the slaves cried worse than a baby what's sick. Most of 'em, however, did their crying on the inside, 'cause if you looked real close you could see the sorrow in their eyes. A few, however, looked like they was dead, but their hearts hadn't got the message yet.

Us Butler plantation slaves used to be the envy of all the slaves in these parts because Master Butler—the first one and then this one—treated their slaves almost like they was family. There's just a few years between me and Master Butler. We was boys together and I taught him to fish and hunt possum. He used to look up to me like I was his big brother. I even saved his life one time. We were down at the river. He was just a little boy and he waded out too far and went under. If I hadn't gone in and gotten him, he would have drowned.

I never dreamed the day would come when he would do something like he's doing. But when the master and the mistress divorced, Mattie said it was going to be bad for us. Didn't think it would get to be this bad.

In a little while the mule wagons will come out

of the barn. They'll be moving real slow, like they know they're carrying slaves to be sold like bales of cotton. A little while after the last of the wagons has left for town, I'll go to the barn and get the coach ready and drive Master into town. I overheard him tell somebody at the auction that by the end of today, four hundred and twenty-nine of us slaves will have been sold.

Don't seem right that us is the ones have to pay the price for another man's weakness.

(Emma, Mattie and Will's daughter, enters.)

MATTIE: *(To Emma.)* Have you gotten
Miss Sarah and Miss Frances dressed that
quick?

EMMA: Master say to let them stay in their
nightclothes and robes for now and to get 'em
dressed after breakfast.

MATTIE: Why he want to wait until then?

EMMA: He say he don't want them spilling food on their good clothes. He's taking them to town to the slave-selling.

MATTIE: He gon' do what? Why he want to take them girls to something like that? He wouldn't do that if the mistress was still here.

emma

I think I miss Mistress Fanny almost as much as Miss Sarah and Miss Frances do. Miss Frances tries to pretend like she don't miss her mama. But I know she does. She's just trying to hide from her feelings. Miss Sarah's not like that. Her feelings know where she is and they find her every night when she goes to bed. It's been almost a year since her mama been gone, but she still cries herself to sleep.

The rain comes down hard as stones. Last night me, Mama, and Papa got soaking wet running back to the quarters. But I was glad for the rain and how loud it was, because I mostly couldn't hear folks crying over the ones what got sold yesterday and the crying of them what's going to be sold today. Seem like there was crying coming from every cabin in the quarters 'cepting ours.

EMMA: *(To Will.)* Papa? What was it like at the slave-selling yesterday?

WILL: Like watching people die. I knew practically every one of them what got sold, knew 'em by face, if not by name. The slave-seller would call 'em up, sometimes a husband and wife together, sometimes a whole family, and sometimes just one. The slave-seller talked so fast, you couldn't understand what he was saying. I guess white folks can listen faster than colored, because the slave-seller be talking fast, and different white folks would raise their hands and the slave-seller would point at first one and shout, "One hundred!" And

then another white man would raise his
hand and the slave-seller would shout, "Two
hundred!" And it would keep on that way
until all of a sudden the slave-seller would
point to a white man and yell, "Sold!" and all
the other white folks would come over and pat
that one on the back and he'd grin and smile
like he'd just bought himself a fine racehorse.

Master say he wasn't going to separate
husbands from wives and parents from their
children. He must've forgot, 'cause he sold
my sister and her husband to a master from
Tennessee, and their daughter was bought by
a lady from Mississippi. The one what bought
my sister didn't even let her come and say
good-bye to me. I watched as her new master
took her away, and when the door closed
behind 'em, I realized that I ain't never
going to see her again. That was like lightning leaping out of a black cloud and striking

me in the chest. The only way I'll ever know she was alive is by this pain in my heart.

(Outside, thunder rolls back and forth across the sky, like the cannon explosions of opposing armies. Will, Mattie, and Emma look up as if they are afraid something is going to come through the ceiling. Then they exchange looks that say they know why Nature is making her presence felt so strongly.)

emma

(After the thunder has passed and there is only the sound of the hard rain.) When Papa told us last night that Aunt Selma, Uncle Bob, and Charlotte had been sold away, I didn't want to believe it. Me and Charlotte was born around the same time. Since neither one of us had a sister, we was sisters to each other. I feel so bad for her. I wonder where she is this morning. Is she in Mississippi already? Is the lady who bought her

nice? Charlotte must be so scared. I know I would be.

mattie

(Steps away from the hot stove and goes to stand in the open kitchen door. She looks through the rain toward the barn. Though it is raining hard she can make out Jenkins, the overseer, bringing slaves from the quarters. The wrists and ankles of the slaves are shackled with iron cuffs and chains that link them to each other.) At mealtimes I stand in the corner of the dining room closest to the kitchen in case Master, one of the girls, or a guest should need me to get something for them. I am as still as the sideboard. Master forgets I'm there, or maybe he don't care. Maybe he think I don't hear and understand what him and the slave-seller say. But I hear. I understood when the slave-seller say: "This is going to be the biggest slave auction ever held in America." He laughed. Master laughed.

When I went back to the quarters that night I told as many as I could that Master was planning to sell most of us. Some folks laughed at me, said Master wouldn't do that. They say he not like other masters.

"He's a good master," Cato said.

I say, "Ain't no such thing! If he was good, he wouldn't be a master."

But George and Rebecca knowed I was telling the truth and that very same night they ran away. Them two been in love since before they was born. Ain't nothing or nobody can separate them. Next morning when Master found out they was gone, he sent Jenkins over to Master Phillips's place to borrow his slave-hunting dogs. All day you could hear them dogs barking and baying through the woods, going this way and that way, trying to sniff out George and Sarah. But that evening them dogs come back with their tongues dragging in the dust. All of us was glad they didn't get caught. But every night since then, Master has had men riding around the plantation all night to make sure nobody else runs away.

Won't need no patrollers tonight 'cause won't be many of us left, just the old people and enough slaves to grow vegetables for food and take care of the animals. But won't be enough to work the cotton and rice.

It's going to be mighty empty in the slave quarters from now on. And mighty quiet. I'm going to miss Junius and the stories he would tell about High John and Brer Rabbit and all the creatures. Wasn't nobody could make me laugh harder than Junius when he got to telling stories. Junius was our preacher, too, and he told us stories from the Good Book, stories that Mistress Kemble had told him, stories about God parting the Red Sea so Moses could lead the slaves away from the Egyptians. Junius going to be telling his stories to different folks from now on and won't nobody be telling us stories. Won't nobody be making music around here either, 'cause Master is gon' sell Ezekiel today. Folks lying in the boneyard want to get up and dance when ol' Ezekiel starts playing that fiddle of his. Ain't gon' be much laughing and dancing around here ever again.

Will comes and stands next to me. He don't look at me and I don't look at him. We just stare into the rain. I can feel him wanting to say something and I want to say something to him but neither one of us knows what it is. Or maybe we know but don't know how to say it. So we just stand here next to each other.

The rain comes down like fiery sorrow.

Interlude I

emma as an old woman

I remember that morning like it was yesterday. I don't know how old I was. I reckon I was around twelve, but nobody kept track of things like that back in slavery. What good would it have done us to know how many years we'd been slaves?

I can still hear the rain. It was so loud we had to almost shout when we had something to say to each other. But wasn't much to say that morning. Or maybe there was a lot to say, but we didn't know the words. Or maybe we was afraid that if we spoke our feelings, nothing but screams would come from our mouths. The rain was so hard and so loud it was like it was doing the grieving for us.

I ain't never seen a rain like that in all the years

since, and that's been a lot of years. I remember my mama telling me that Granny Wilma say she'd never seen rain like that in all her years. She was the oldest slave on the Butler plantation and had known Master's granddaddy, who was the one that started the plantation. If you put all the years of Granny Wilma's remembering together with all my years of remembering, that's a lot of years. My granddaughter, Jessie Mae, can read, write, and do numbers, and she say that would probably be close to two hundred years. That was some rain!

All my children and grandchildren got their education. I would've turned 'em out of the house if they hadn't. Every day when they came home from school I had them tell me different things out of their books. I remember one time when Sarah, my oldest girl, told me that in one of her books it said a picture is worth a thousand words.

I told her whoever wrote that didn't know very much. When I think back on slavery and all what happened that day when God cried, couldn't no picture make you feel what it was like. Maybe a picture could show you the rain, but that picture couldn't make you feel how thick and heavy the air was and how hard it was to breathe. That picture couldn't make you feel how our skin was covered with a sweat that was like grease that had been used too many times to fry chicken in.

If you had a picture of the dining room that morning you would see a long table covered with a white cloth, the china place settings and silverware and Master, the slave-seller, and Master's two daughters seated around the table. You'd see me and Mama going back and forth bringing in the breakfast of grits, fried apples, pancakes, syrup, sausage, and coffee. But you wouldn't smell the odors from everyone's bodies. That picture wouldn't let you smell the mold coming from the walls. You'd see me and Mama in that picture and we would look like we wasn't feeling a thing.

That picture would be a lie.

2

The Dining Room

master

Today is the last day, thank God! I don't know
what I'd do if I had to stand in that barn for a
third day and watch my slaves being sold off. I've
known a lot of them since I was a boy. I played
with some of them when I was growing up. When
a lot of them jumped the broom and got married,
I was there with a bottle of rum as a wedding
present. I was there when a lot of the younger
ones were born. This is the hardest thing I've
ever had to do. But it's not like I had any choice
in the matter. It's either sell off my slaves and
pay my gambling debts or go to prison.

I want to tell them how sorry I am to have to
do this. But I don't know if it would matter to
them. I see them standing on the auction block

and I wonder what they're thinking, what they're feeling. Some of them cry, but most don't show any emotion. Their faces are as blank as tree bark.

They probably aren't feeling anything. That's one of the ways niggers are different from white people. Their emotions are not as refined as ours. Things that would hurt a white man or woman don't affect them. If anybody tried to take my Sarah or Frances away from me, I think I would kill them. Their mother thought she could take them from me. By the time my lawyers got through with her she was grateful I allowed her to see the girls for two months every year.

My girls! Frances is better than any son I could have had. She's only nine, but she's full of questions about the plantation and how to manage niggers. By the time she's of age to marry I plan to have this place back to what it was when my father passed it on to me and I'll pass it on to her.

She is excited to be going to the auction today.

I wish I could say the same about Sarah. She may be a year older than her sister, but she acts much younger. She sits there with her arms folded across her chest and hasn't touched the food on her plate. That look of disapproval on her face reminds me of her mother. I don't need those accusing eyes anywhere near me today.

MASTER: *(To Mattie.)* I'm taking Emma with me today to look after Sarah.

mattie

I am clearing the table and almost drop the bowl of fried apples when Master says he is taking Emma with him today.

Us slaves' survival depends on us knowing what the white folks are thinking. Sometimes we know what they're thinking before they do, but I didn't know Master was planning on taking Emma today. Me and him is almost like sister and brother because my mama was his wet-nurse. I hope he ain't forgot that.

I look at the slave-seller sitting beside Master Butler. There's a toothpick sticking out of the left corner of his mouth. He takes a sip of coffee without moving that toothpick out of the way. He eats with that toothpick bobbing up and down. I wish he'd stop looking at Emma like she's a hog and he's trying to figure how many pork chops and slabs of bacon he can get out of her.

slave-seller

After today my reputation will spread all across the South. By this time next year I'll have offices in New Orleans, Mobile, and Charleston. Ain't no other auctioneer in the South could have gotten as good a price for slaves as the ones I got yesterday. Word will get around among the slave owners that George Weems is the man to go to if you want to get the most money for your slaves.

Auctioning slaves is like auctioning anything else—cotton, cattle, sorghum molasses, or sugarcane. You have to make your buyers believe they're getting the very best merchandise there is. It doesn't have to *be* the best. You just have to make them *think* it's the best. If the buyer is convinced he's getting the best, he'll gladly pay more.

Now. Take that girl there what's clearing the table. Young girl like that who can cook and care for children? She's worth four, five hundred dollars easy, maybe more. Coming back from the auction yesterday I asked Butler about putting her on the block. He said she wasn't for sale. We'll see about that. Money is money, and if he's selling all his slaves except twenty-one, he must need a lot of it. Word is that he's about the worst card player to ever sit down at a table, which is why he's such a popular man when the cards are being dealt. I bet if I talk around among the folks who come to the auction today I can find somebody who'd pay a lot for a girl like that. Once I dangle the promise of some more hard, cold dollars in front of Butler's eyes, I'll see what he has to say then.

sarah

If Mama was here I wouldn't have to go see the slaves get sold away. She and Papa used to argue all the time about the slaves. She wanted Papa to let them go free. One time I heard them arguing and Mama said she would never have married Papa if she had known he owned slaves. Papa said whether he owned slaves was none of her business. He said she was a woman and her business was taking care of the house and the children. Mama said if that's all he thought a woman was good for he had married the wrong one.

Mama was an actress in England before she married Papa. That's where she was born and grew up. Mama said they didn't have slavery in England or anywhere in Europe. I wish I was in

England right this minute. Then I wouldn't have to go to the auction. But Emma will be with me. Papa doesn't want me with him and Frances. I don't want to be with them, either.

frances

I'm glad Papa said Emma's coming to be with Sarah. That means I'll have Papa all to myself. He says I'm like him and Sarah is like Mama. I miss Mama, but I don't miss hearing her and Papa arguing all the time. I'm glad she's not here today, because I know she and Papa would be arguing about him taking me to the auction.

Papa said the plantation will be mine one day. He says his Papa started teaching him all he needed to know when he was about my age, so it's time for me to start learning, too. But I don't think there's going to be much for me to learn, because after today we won't have many slaves. But Papa said he will not gamble anymore and that he's going to build the plantation back up.

I'm glad Papa didn't take me to the auction yesterday. That's when Ovid was sold away. Ovid was teaching me how to ride a horse. Papa said no one I know is being sold today. At supper last night Mister Weems said you can't let your feelings get in the way of business. I suppose he's right. Mama would go down to the quarters and talk with the slaves like they were her friends. Papa would tell her not to, but she would anyway. Papa said she was spoiling the slaves, that she was making them lazy. Papa said the slaves were lazy enough without any help from her.

Ovid wasn't lazy. Or maybe he was and I was too young to see it. I hope Papa will teach me how to tell when a slave is being lazy and when he isn't.

MASTER: *(To slave-seller.)* I wish this infernal rain would stop! A man can't think straight with that constant racket. I heard that Clive

Howard was trying to get a jump on the other plantation owners and had his slaves put cottonseed in the ground last week.

SLAVE-SELLER: How many acres?

MASTER: Two thousand or so.

SLAVE-SELLER: He's a ruined man, 'cause that seed is swimming away from here.

MASTER: There's all kinds of gambling, I guess. I gambled on cards and lost and now I've got to pay up. But gambling on the weather, that's the worst gamble there is. Sometimes I wish my family had never gotten into this business. You gamble on the weather trying to figure out the best time to put your seed in the ground. Then you gamble again trying to know when is the best time to pick the cotton. My papa told me about the time he delayed picking cotton from one week to the next and what happened? A day or so before he was going to start picking, the temperature dropped and there come a hailstorm. Hail came down so hard and so fast it broke every cotton plant like you break a matchstick. Destroyed the entire crop.

And if taking your chances on the weather isn't bad enough, you have to watch your slaves to make sure the work gets done when it's supposed to. You look away from them for a minute and they'll stop working. Sometimes I wonder who owns who. The law says I own them, but as much grief as they cause me, I sometimes think they own me.

SLAVE-SELLER: You ain't the first owner I've heard say something like that. If you don't mind my asking, what're your plans once the auction is done?

MASTER: I'll be moving back to Philadelphia, where I have a house. I need to get away from here for a while. I know that much. This selling business has been hard on me. Some of the slaves look at me like they think I'm Satan himself. It's not like I want to sell 'em. If they think I'm enjoying this, they don't know a thing about me. I wouldn't be doing this if I had a choice in the matter.

slave-seller

(Takes a last noisy sip of coffee.) I don't have much respect for a man who wants to cry over some niggers. Man like that don't deserve to own slaves. Why does he care what they think? If he sold some of his mules, he wouldn't care what the mule thought, because a mule can't think. Niggers ain't no different. And to tell the truth, I've seen some mules that had more sense.

SLAVE-SELLER: *(To Master.)* Well, it's time for me to get on into town and make sure everything's in order. Just a few more hours and you'll be a wealthy man, Mr. Butler.

MASTER: Thank God for that! How's your voice? You sound a little hoarse this morning.

SLAVE-SELLER: I'll be fine. Having to shout so loud to be heard over the rain strained my voice a little, but I'm fine. See you shortly. *(He leaves.)*

MASTER: *(To Emma.)* Go get the girls ready. I want to leave soon.

Interlude II

slave-seller as an old man

I remember that day like it was just last week. My God, how it rained. That rain came down like a waterfall. It was already hot in that barn and the heat coming off all the people crammed in there—slave owners and slaves—made it worse. Sweat poured off everybody like grease off a hog at a pig roast. And if the heat wasn't bad enough, the sound of the rain on the roof of that stable was so loud I had to yell to make myself heard.

I thought that auction was going to make my repu-tation, that I would be in so much demand, I'd have slave auction houses all across the South. But later that same year the economy went bad and the price of cotton dropped something fierce. The plantation

owners needed to raise money and all they had to sell
was slaves, but with everybody wanting to sell, wasn't
hardly nobody in a position to buy.

Not that it would've mattered much to me. By the
time the auction was done, damned if I hadn't lost my
voice. I figured it would come back to me after a few
days of rest, so I went on home to Memphis and waited
for my voice to return. A week passed. Two weeks. Then
a month and another month. Finally I went to a doctor
and he said I'd ruined my vocal box, that all the
screaming and yelling I'd done had put too great a
strain on my voice and wasn't nothing he could do to
bring it back.

What could I do with a voice that was no more than
a whisper? I sure as hell couldn't auction off anybody's
slaves even if there'd been anybody to buy them. I tried
to get jobs being overseer on a plantation, but niggers
don't obey overseers even when they shout. They would
laugh at one whose voice could hardly be heard when he
whispered in your ear. I couldn't do nothing but go back

to Arkansas and work on the little farm my brother and I had inherited from our parents.

Then, in sixty-one, the War started. I joined up the next year, but in my first battle, the one at Vicksburg, I took a bullet in the leg. Gangrene set in and I lost the leg. I guess it could've been worse. The fellow standing next to me took a bullet in the chest and I reckon he was dead before he hit the ground. Confederate Army didn't have no place for a dead man or a one-legged man, especially if he couldn't talk above a whisper. So I come on back here and this is where I been ever since. About all my brother and I can grow in this rocky soil is veg-etables for ourselves. Some years we have enough to eat and some years we don't.

I never did marry. What woman wants a man with only one leg? About the only folks who don't care if a man's got one leg or two is the Ku Klux Klan, a bunch of good ol' boys what joined up together to keep the niggers from taking over everything. I can't ride with the boys when they go out and set fire to the house of some nigger boy who's gotten too big for his britches, but I enjoy hearing them talk about all the things they do to scare niggers.

I try and tell some of the young people about how it was before the War, about how I auctioned off more slaves at one time than anybody ever had, but they don't want to hear about it. I guess can't nobody see who you used to be. All they can see is what's in front of their eyes and they look at me and see an old man who talks in a whisper and has only one leg and who, if somebody pushed him over, couldn't get up off the floor by himself. What use is a hoarse cripple?

3

Upstairs

emma

Up here in the girls' room the roof is right above our heads and the rain sounds like a lot of people are pounding nails as fast as they can. But the rain on the windows makes a higher sound, like grains of corn being shaken in a jar. Frances says something to me. I see her mouth moving, but I cannot hear what she is saying. I go to her and bend over so she can speak directly in my ear.

FRANCES: Brush my hair!

EMMA: I brushed it when you got up this morning. It looks very pretty.

FRANCES: I want you to brush it again.

EMMA: Miss Frances, your hair don't need no more brushing.

FRANCES: Do it, Emma!

emma

I take the brush from the top of the bureau and begin brushing her hair, slowly, gently. She has never spoken to me like I'm a dog that she can make sit and stay put on her say-so. Her mama would've slapped her face if she'd heard her speak to me like that. *(Emma's thoughts are interrupted by the sound of crying. Emma stops brushing Frances's hair and turns to see Sarah sitting on the edge of her bed with her head down.)*

EMMA: What's the matter, Miss Sarah?
FRANCES: There's nothing the matter with her.
   She's just a crybaby.
SARAH: I'm not!
FRANCES: Are too!
SARAH: Not!
FRANCES: Are!

sarah

The rocking chair Mother used to sit in and read to us is in the corner of the room. I grab Emma's hand and pull her over to the chair. She sits down. I sit on her lap, put my head on her chest and put my arms around her and we start rocking. She holds me tight like Mama used to. I hold on to her like there's nobody left in the world except us. No one else here knows what it's like to be me except Emma. Not Papa. And certainly not Frances. Maybe that's why Mama left. Maybe being with Papa made her feel too lonely.

FRANCES: *(Loudly.)* Emma! You didn't finish brushing my hair.

EMMA: Miss Sarah needs me now.

Interlude III

frances butler as an old woman

I remember that morning. I remember the way Emma said, "Miss Sarah needs me now," as if nothing else in the world mattered except what Sarah needed. I wanted to say, I need you, too. And God knows I did.

I was trying so hard to be who Papa wanted me to be, but I was only nine years old. How could I take my mother's place? I wanted to be everything to Papa that Mama hadn't been. But he loved cards even more than he loved me.

He didn't play cards for a long time after the auction. We moved to Philadelphia and lived reasonably well after Papa paid off his gambling debts. Sarah and I went to the finest finishing school. However, slowly, Papa slipped back into the cards, and the next thing we knew, silverware, silver candlesticks, Grandmother's jewelry, and the like were taken from the house to pay off all the money he was losing at the card tables of his so-called gentlemen friends.

Perhaps it is just as well Papa died soon after he resumed his love affair with cards. I am still thankful that he did not have to live to see our country go to war over the slaves.

Sarah married a Philadelphia lawyer. I ended up marrying an English minister, of all people, a gentleman I met while visiting Mother once. Though English, he shared my sentiments about slavery and slaves, and after the War we returned to the Butler plantation. It had always been my dream to restore it to the glory it had enjoyed during my great-grandfather's time. Alas, that was not to be. If the slaves were difficult to manage when they were slaves, they were impossible after the war that set them free.

I might have had an easier time of it if it hadn't been for George and Rebecca. I didn't remember them at first

*until, with great glee, they told me they had run off when
they learned Papa was planning to sell most of his slaves.
Then I recalled Papa mentioning them from time to time
and wondering what had happened to them. I'm certain
he had no idea that they had survived for all those years.
It seems they found a cave, set up house in it, and even
had a child. When I asked them what they did for food,
they said Mattie and Will had brought food out to them
almost every day. I couldn't believe my ears! I thought
Mattie and Will were the most faithful slaves we owned.
If either one of them had still been there I think I would
have run them off the place for being so disloyal. But
they had left the place right after the War ended. George
told me they went to Kentucky. I wondered why they went
there but didn't care enough to try and find out.*

    *George and Rebecca made my life impossible with all
their talk about the rights of Negroes! They wanted to
vote, and they wanted to be paid wages, and they wanted
schools and hospitals. Arthur, my husband, and I had no
tolerance for niggers thinking they were the equal of*

whites and after a few years we sold the plantation and said good riddance.

I don't know why I still remember that morning, but I think about it sometimes. Maybe I'd never felt like I needed anybody the way I felt I needed Emma that morning. Even though Sarah was sitting in her lap, I went over and stood next to the rocking chair. Somehow, Emma found space for me. She wasn't a big girl, but that morning her lap seemed plenty big.

She put an arm around me and hugged me as tightly as she was hugging Sarah. We rocked back and forth in that chair while the rain slammed against the roof and the windows as if it was trying to break in. Sometimes I think I could have stayed like that for the rest of my life.

I don't know how much time passed, but suddenly we heard Papa calling up the stairs that it was time to go. Emma hurried and got us dressed and took us down and left us standing by the front door while she went back to the kitchen.

I don't know why, but I wanted to cry.

4

The Kitchen

mattie

Emma stands just inside the kitchen door. Her large, round eyes seem bigger than usual. I want to take her in my arms and hug her to me, but if I do, my tears will be as great as the rain. My tears would be like that rain God sent when he destroyed the world back in Noah's time. So, I stand here by the stove looking at my only child and she stands there by the door looking at me and the rain comes down like it wants to kill us all.

emma

Mama and I look at each other like we want to stamp the other's likeness on our brains. She stands there in front of the stove. Her skin is as soft and black as night. Her hands are big and the veins stand out on the back of them. I don't have to feel them to know that the inside of her hands have calluses as thick and hard as a slab of wood.

MASTER: *(Entering the kitchen.)* Ah! Here you are. It's time for us to be going, Emma. Mattie, some of the ladies and gentlemen from the auction will be coming back with me this evening. Get several of the hams that are curing in the barn and champagne from the cellar. We'll have yams and rice and greens and a bread pudding for dessert.

MATTIE: Yes, sir. Master?

MASTER: What is it, Mattie?

MATTIE: I was just wondering if Miss Sarah wouldn't be happier staying here with Emma today. She's delicate, and seeing a slave-selling, well—sir, you know how the littlest thing can upset her and make her sick.

MASTER: And that's precisely why I want her to

go. It's time she started growing up. She's a year older than Frances, but acts like she's a baby.

MATTIE: Yes, sir.

master

I know what she is thinking, what they are both thinking. Coming back from the auction yesterday Weems asked me if I'd be interested if he could get a good price for Emma. I told him no, but I said it in such a way that Weems knew I meant maybe.

Emma acts too much like she's the girls' mother. Sarah, especially, pays more heed to Emma than she does me. Just last month I heard Sarah crying in her sleep and went in to comfort her. She shrank back from my touch like she thought I was going to hurt her. I reached for her again, to hold her in my arms, and she said, "I want Emma! Get Emma!" And in the middle of the night I had to go down to the quarters and get Emma. Emma no more than walked into the girls' room and Sarah stopped crying, held out her arms, and wrapped them tightly around Emma.

I will not have my oldest daughter turn into a copy of her mother. I won't!

emma

I look at Mama. Mama looks at me. Master touches me on the shoulder. Before I know it I am walking through the passageway that connects the kitchen to the house. I look back and see Mama standing in the kitchen door. And then I go into the house and toward the front door, where Miss Sarah and Miss Frances wait.

Interlude IV

master

(Shortly before his death.)

Despite the rain the auction was a success. I made a little over $300,000. I was able to pay my gambling debts and the auctioneer's commission and still have enough left to live comfortably. So I took the girls to Philadelphia and never went back to the plantation. I didn't plan it that way. It just happened. I had left Jenkins in charge and he was a good plantation manager. Not enough slaves remained to grow rice or cotton, so he rented out most of the land to other plantation owners. Twice a year he sent me reports and a check. It's not like I would've been able to do any better if I'd been there.

But selling off my slaves was a bittersweet experience. I had no choice, but knowing that I had squandered what my grandfather and father had built and passed on to me, well, that's been hard to live with.

And then there's Sarah. She's a mother with children of her own now, a girl named Emma and a boy named Owen. But she's never forgiven me. That look of disapproval I saw in her eyes the last day of the auction has not softened. I've told her countless times how sorry I was, that I wish things could have been different, that I cared about my slaves more than she thinks I did. But regardless of what I say, nothing changes her feelings toward me.

I disappointed Frances too. The plantation was to have been her inheritance. And it will be, but nothing remains except a few old slaves and a house and barn that are probably ready to fall down. She tells me it doesn't matter, that she will return the Butler plantation to its former glory.

I admire her spirit, but I think the glory days of the Butler plantation are only a memory now. Times are changing and not for the better, if you ask my opinion. There is a growing sentiment against slavery in the

North. Some want to free the slaves and get rid of slavery entirely. Then what? Do they want niggers living next door to them? Do they want niggers going to school with white children? Do they want niggers marrying their daughters?

Slavery has been the best thing that's happened to niggers because it has helped civilize them, as much as that is possible given their limited intelligence. Slavery has also built America. Rather than ending slavery, we need to expand slavery westward from the South to the shores of the Pacific Ocean and down into Mexico. With slavery, America will become prosperous and strong. Without it, well, I shudder to think what will become of our nation.

There are some whisperings that the matter will have to be decided in a war between the North and the South. I can't believe Yankees would be so wrongheaded as to go to war over niggers! If that ever comes about, I hope I will be resting peacefully in my grave. It would break my heart to see the Southern way of life destroyed.

5

The Slave Auction

(The stable where the slave auction takes place.)

emma

The ride in the coach from the plantation to here made me feel sick in my stomach. The coach rocked from side to side and up and down as it bounced in and out of all the holes the rain has made in the road. The rain was so loud on the coach, nobody talked. I sat on one side next to Sarah. Frances sat on the other side next to Master Butler. Sarah leaned against me, the thumb of one hand in her mouth. With the other she held on to my hand hard, like she's still doing. My hand hurts, but I don't have the heart to ask her to let go.

I've never been in a place like this. It's like a barn but only bigger, a lot bigger than the one at the plantation. Along the sides are stalls where the horses are kept, 'cept there're no horses in the stalls today. Slaves are packed in them tight like cotton in bales.

In the center of the stable there's a platform. I guess that's where the slave-seller will be when the selling starts. There's a lot of finely dressed white folks standing around talking among themselves. There's even a few women in big, wide dresses.

Master is walking around shaking hands with different ones. The men laugh and pat him on the back like he has done something good. He points down at Frances, who is holding his other hand. The men bend over and shake hands with her. She does a little curtsy and grins from ear to ear.

sarah

It is hot in the stable and it smells like hay and horses and sweat. Nobody seems to notice or care. Everyone is laughing and talking like they're at a Christmas ball. There's Frances acting like she's a princess with her little curtsy. A man bows and kisses her hand. I wish people liked me as much as they like her.

I pull Emma toward the door at the other end of the barn. I want to be as far away from everything as I can.

(Near the center of the stable.)

MASTER: Why, Mr. and Mrs. Denman! So good of you to come, especially in this awful weather we're having.

DENMAN: Pierce, it would take more than some rain to keep us away from an auction of the Butler plantation slaves. If every slave owner took care of his slaves the way you do, even folks in Boston would say that a society based on slavery is the highest form of civilization.

MASTER: That's kind of you to say, Rodney.

THE SLAVE AUCTION

(In another part of the stable.)

SLAVE BUYER 1: *(To another buyer.)* I don't like to
take advantage of another man's misfortune,
but when that man brings misfortune on himself because the sound of a deck of cards being
shuffled is like music to him, well—

SLAVE BUYER 2: I agree wholeheartedly. I've
had the pleasure myself of relieving Pierce
of some of his money at the card table. Well,
I should be truthful and say, a lot of his
money. *(Laughs.)* I like Pierce, but when it
comes to cards, the man is a fool.

(At the stalls.)

SLAVE BUYER 3: *(To a slave in a stall.)* Boy! You!
Come here!

SLAVE 1: You mean me, suh?

SLAVE BUYER 3: Yes, you! Come here! *(Slave 1*

squeezes through the slaves packed in the stall and makes his way to the front.) Open your mouth, boy! *(Slave Buyer 3 takes a pair of white gloves from his coat pocket, puts them on and then rubs his fingers over the gums and teeth of Slave 1. He squeezes the slave's arms and then his thighs.)* I think you'll do fine, boy. Just fine!

(In a stall.)

SLAVE 2: See that man there?

SLAVE 3: Which one?

SLAVE 2: The one with the long black cane.

SLAVE 4: I see him.

SLAVE 3: Oh, I see him now.

SLAVE 2: I hope Master don't sell none of us to him. He looks like the kind what eats a slave before breakfast every morning.

SLAVE 5: How can you tell?

SLAVE 2: Look at his mouth. See how it droops

down. And look at them tiny eyes. I can just tell. That man is hard on slaves!

SLAVE 4: He do look like it would give him pleasure to buy one of us just so he could have someone to beat on.

SLAVE 3: But look at the man heading over here. I wouldn't mind if he bought me.

SLAVE 1: He has a pleasant-enough face, but just because somebody looks nice it don't mean he is.

SLAVE 3: I know, but I'd rather take my chances with one that looks like he won't take the lash to me.

(The slave buyer just referred to approaches the stall where the slaves have been talking.)

SLAVE 3: *(Shouting.)* Master! Master! If you looking for a young, strong field hand, I'm your boy! Yes, suh! Come here, Master, and feel the muscles in these arms. *(Slave Buyer 4 stops and looks at*

Slave 3. He feels his arms and shoulders.) I can work from sunup to moondown if I have to and then work some more. Yes, suh! *(Waves frantically toward the back of the pen and a young woman hurries forward.)* This here is my wife. She can work as good and hard as me. Yes, suh! She sho' can! If you buy us, Master, you'll never be sorry. We'll see to that!

SLAVE BUYER 4: *(Smiling.)* What's your name, boy?

SLAVE 3: Bob, suh. And this here is my wife. Her name is Mary. Bob and Mary.

SLAVE BUYER 4: *(His words are directed at Bob, but as he talks he stares, up and down, at Mary.)* I like a boy who takes initiative, who doesn't sit back and wait to see what his fate is going to be. I think you'll fit in well at my plantation. You— and your wife!

BOB: Yes, suh! I know we will, suh! Thank you

very much! *(Slave Buyer 4 walks away).*

MARY: *(To Bob, concerned.)* I didn't like the way that man was looking at me.

BOB: What're you talking about? He wasn't looking at you in no particular way. Everything's gon' be all right. Trust me. If that man buys us, we'll be all right.

MARY: I hope so.

(In another part of the stable.)

SLAVE-SELLER: *(Whispering to a lady in a long, pale blue dress.)* Mrs. Henfield, I believe you told me that you need a girl to look after your daughter?

MISTRESS HENFIELD: Why, yes. But I don't see any such girl in your catalog of slaves to be sold today.

SLAVE-SELLER: No, ma'am, there isn't. But I

know of such a girl and if you were to offer
the right amount, I believe Mister Butler
could be convinced to part with the girl.
She's very experienced and has been taking
care of Mister Butler's two daughters this
past year.

MISTRESS HENFIELD: She sounds perfect. Are
you sure Mister Butler will part with such a
valuable girl?

SLAVE-SELLER: He is planning to move back
to his place in Philadelphia with his daughters.
I would think he would be able to hire an up-
standing white woman to care for his children
there, one he would pay and not have to worry
about feeding and clothing, too.

MISTRESS HENFIELD: I understand what
you're saying. Perhaps you'll speak with
Pierce on my behalf and inquire if he has any
interest in selling the girl.

SLAVE-SELLER: I'll be happy to, Mrs. Henfield.

THE SLAVE AUCTION

(At the rear of the stable.)

emma

I look over at the stalls. There's Aunt Hagar.
Whoever buys her better look out, 'cause she can
fight just as good as a man and maybe better. She
ain't that big, but that don't matter none. Even
Jenkins, the overseer, is scared of her. One time
he told her to do something and she say she do it
tomorrow and he say, naw, he wants it done right
now and she say, "Tomorrer," and turn and walk
away and ol' Jenkins didn't do a thing. He just
stood there and stared after her. And he didn't
give her no whupping either.

There's Joe! He's a little older than me.
Somebody told me that he was sweet on me.
Maybe he is, but with him working in the field
and me working in the house, I don't know for
myself if he like me and how much. Many nights
I don't get back to the quarters from the big

house until everyone's asleep. That's how it's been, especially since the mistress left. I spend many a night sleeping in the girls' room 'cause Miss Sarah be crying so hard about her mama leaving. Joe is going to be sold today and I'll never know if he was sweet on me or if I would've been sweet on him. A white lady in a long blue dress walks over to the stall where he is. She looks at him. He doesn't look back at her. He's just staring straight ahead, his face as blank as the boards of this barn. I wonder what he's looking at. I wonder what he's seeing.

A few of the slaves look like they want to kill somebody. Most of 'em though look like they not here. If I was going to be sold away I think that's what I would look like. I would be trying to get ready for whatever was going to happen to me. I would be angry later.

SLAVE-SELLER: *(Bangs gavel loudly on table, then shouts in a loud but raspy voice.)* Gentlemen! And

THE SLAVE AUCTION

I see a few ladies, also. May I have your attention, please? Your attention, please?

Thank you. My name is George Weems, and I'd appreciate it if you would remember that name and tell all your friends that when it comes to selling slaves, nobody can do it better than George Weems. *(Applause.)*

It is my honor and privilege to preside on this, the last day of the greatest auction of slaves in American history! *(More applause.)*

And, I will add, that not only is this the largest auction of slaves, this is also the finest slave auction in American history! What we have here today are slaves who have been kept as if they were thoroughbred horses. They've been well fed; they're strong; they're obedient. And they love to serve their white folks! That's because there's no finer manager of slaves anywhere in the South than Mr. Pierce Butler. *(Slave-seller points to Pierce Butler, who is standing near the back of the barn. Butler grins, waves to the crowd, which applauds him vigorously. But the sound of the applause can scarcely be heard over the rain pounding on the roof.)*

He has a reputation for being a man who treats his slaves almost as good as he treats his children. Not only are they well fed, they've never been whipped or beaten, except when they deserve it, of course. *(Laughter.)*

You have never seen such a fine-looking group of slaves and I doubt you ever will again. Before we begin, I'd like to remind you gentlemen—and ladies—of the terms of the sale: one third cash today, and the remainder in two equal annual installments. And now, let the auction begin!

(More applause and a few sounds of cheering. Slave-seller nods at a young white man about eighteen years of age, who goes to a stall and

THE SLAVE AUCTION

brings out a man, woman, and two small children and leads them onto the small platform.)

SLAVE-SELLER: If you will turn your attention to your catalogs we will be starting today with lot number ninety-eight, a family of four: George, around age twenty-seven; his wife, Sue, twenty-six; and their two children, George and Harry. This is a fine family, young, obviously good procreators, who will undoubtedly enrich your holdings with more healthy and fit slave children. Turn around, George, so the gentlemen—and ladies—can see how strong and able you are. *(When George is slow to move, the slave-seller takes him by the shoulders and walks him around in a small circle.)*

When you buy a family like this, young and able and fruitful, you're also buying yourself a new generation of slaves. They are to be sold as a family and I want to start the bidding at seven hundred and fifty dollars.

Who'll give me eight? Do I hear eight, eight, eight, if you bid eight you won't be late! Ha! I've got eight over here from the gentleman in the red tie. Can I get nine, nine hundred, nine, nine, nine, I want nine, nine would be so fine. Ha! Nine hundred from my good friend, Mr. Powell from Atlanta, a man who knows how to judge flesh when he sees it, but I know you gentlemen aren't going to let him get away with these four slaves for a mere nine hundred dollars. If you let him do that then he's nothing but a thief and we know Mr. Powell wouldn't steal four fine slaves like these from his friends. *(Loud laughter.)*

I've got a thousand, one thousand dollars from the gentleman to my left. . . .

emma

The slave-seller talk so fast I can't always make

out what he saying, but I reckon I understand all I need to understand and that's the numbers— twelve hundred, thirteen, fourteen. Miss Fanny had started teaching me numbers before she went away and I know fourteen is bigger than thirteen.

Finally fewer and fewer folks call out numbers until it gets quiet. Then the slave-seller say, "Going once! Going twice! Going three times! Gone! Sold to Mr. Powell from Atlanta for two thousand four hundred dollars." Then the slave-seller bangs a mallet on the table and everybody claps their hands.

SLAVE-SELLER: If you'd step right up here, Mr. Powell, my clerk will be happy to take your money and the information we need so we can give you an official bill of sale. And we thank you. I know you'll be very happy with this family you just bought.

We turn now to numbers ninety-nine, one hundred, one hundred one, and one hundred two. We have here Kate's John, around age thirty-one, who works rice and is a prime man; his Betsey, around age twenty, who also works rice, but is a little soft in the head; and their two children, Kate, age six, and Violet, who is three months. I know you gentlemen will not be put off by Betsey not being quite right in the head. You're not buying her for her brains but for her muscles, and you can see she's a big, strapping girl who can work hard and won't give nobody no trouble. I'll entertain an opening bid of five hundred dollars.

emma

The selling goes fast. As soon as one group is sold, the slave-seller calls the names of the next ones and on and on it goes. In between each group of slaves being sold, the rain seems to get louder and louder. That makes the slave-seller have to shout louder and louder, but the louder he try to shout, the hoarser his voice gets. It's like the rain is trying to drown him. But don't seem like nothing this day is going to stop him from selling slaves.

Number 103—Wooster, age 45; field hand
   and fair mason
Number 104—Mary, age 40; cotton hand
Sold for $300 each.
Number 105—Commodore Bob, aged; rice hand
Number 106—Kate, aged; cotton
Number 107—Linda, age 19; cotton, prime young
   woman
Number 108—Joe, 13; rice, prime boy
Sold for $600 each.
Number 109—Bob, 30; rice
Number 110—Mary, 25; rice, prime woman
Sold for $1,135 each.

Number 111—Anson, 49; ruptured, one eye

Number 112—Violet, 55; rice hand

Sold for $250 each

emma

Anson. He only got one eye. Papa say long time ago when Anson was young, Master Butler and another owner decided to have a contest to see whose slave was the best fighter. Master put Anson in the fight and his eye ended up on the fists of the slave from the other plantation.

As the slave-seller calls the names of each slave I say his or her name to myself. Since I work in the house I don't know a lot of them, but that don't matter. I want to remember what they look like because won't nobody here ever see any of them again.

Number 113—Allen Jeffrey, 46; rice hand and

   sawyer in steam mill

Number 114—Sikey, 43; rice hand

Number 115—Watty, 5; infirm legs

Sold for $250 each

Number 116—Rina, 18; rice, prime young woman

Number 117—Lena, 1

Sold for $645 each

Number 118—Pompey, 31; rice; lame in one foot

Number 119—Kitty, 30; rice, prime young woman

Number 120—Pompey, Jr., 10; prime boy

Number 121—John, 7

Number 122—Noble, 1; boy

Sold for $580 each

emma

It's not going to be hard to remember anybody's face because everybody is wearing the same one. Their mouths are set in a straight line. Their eyes look straight ahead and over the crowd. It's not like there's something they're looking at, but more like they've closed their eyes while keeping them open.

If it was me up there I would try not to think about what was happening. I would try not to think about anything. I would try to disappear from everybody, including myself, and that way I wouldn't feel anything. It would be like it wasn't me that was being sold but somebody who just looked like me. I would be somewhere else. I'd hide in the sound of the rain pounding on the roof like the hooves of frightened horses.

sarah

All I can see is the backs of the people, but I can hear Mr. Weems calling out the names of the slaves, and then he talks very fast until he bangs his gavel on the table, and then he calls out the names of some more slaves. I can't see Papa and Frances from here. Frances is probably enjoying herself. I want to go home. The rain is falling even harder now. It's like God is angry at Papa for what he's doing.

THE SLAVE AUCTION

SLAVE-SELLER: I want to take a second to thank you gentlemen—and ladies—for your lively bidding. We're moving along at a good clip. I would like to call your attention now to chattel number three hundred and nineteen, Jeffrey, a twenty-three-year-old buck, who is a prime cotton hand. When this boy is around at cotton-picking time the cotton just seems to jump out of the bolls and into his sack. Jeffrey comes by himself, no wife or children, so I'm expecting a good price for this boy. I'll start the bidding at a thousand dollars.

emma

Jeffrey's face is different from the others. He is staring over the heads of the men bidding on him, but his eyes are looking around, searching for someone. There! He's found who he was looking for. I follow his stare to the stalls, where I see a girl. I ain't never seen two people look at each other like they're doing. It's like they're trying to hug each other with their eyes. "Sold to Mr. Ellington from Mobile for one thousand three hundred and ten dollars." And the slave-seller goes *BANG!* on the table with his mallet.

JEFFREY: *(As he is led from the platform to his new master.)* Master Ellington, suh! Could I have a word with you?

ELLINGTON: What's on your mind, boy?

JEFFREY: Thank you, suh! You look like a good man, suh, one what fear God. There's a girl, her name is Dorcas, suh, and the Lawd knows that I love her more than anything on earth and she loves me and I will never love anybody the way I do her. Please buy her, Master Ellington, suh! We love each other so much.

ELLINGTON: Well, that's very nice, boy, but I'm

a businessman and I can't be throwing my money around for the sake of love.

JEFFREY: Oh, it wouldn't be like that, Master Ellington. No, suh! Wouldn't be like that at all! Dorcas, she a prime woman. Oh, yes suh! She tall, got long arms, she strong and healthy and she can work all day. Yes, suh! She one of the best rice hands on the whole plantation. She be a bargain, suh!

ELLINGTON: Well, let me see her.

JEFFREY: *(Leads Ellington over to the slave stall where Dorcas stands.)* This is her!

ELLINGTON: *(Looks Dorcas over carefully.)* Turn around, Dorcas. *(As she does so, Ellington nods approvingly.)* Take that rag off your head. *(Dorcas removes the colorful handkerchief from her head and Ellington examines her scalp for any signs of wounds or disease. Then he feels her arms and looks at her teeth.)* All right, boy. I believe she *would* be a bargain.

JEFFREY: Yes, suh! Oh yes, suh! She a bargain all right.

ELLINGTON: I'll buy her.

JEFFREY: *(Smiling for the first time.)* Oh, Master Ellington! Thank you so much, suh! Thank you so much! There ain't gon' be no two harder-working niggers on your plantation, suh!

SLAVE-SELLER: *(Brings Dorcas to the platform.)* We will now move on to chattel number three-forty-five, seventeen years old, can pick cotton so fast you think she's using her toes as well as her fingers. This is a prime woman, gentleman, no children, but you can look at those hips and see she's built for birth. I'll accept bids starting at seven hundred and fifty dollars.

ELLINGTON: Eight hundred!

SLAVE-SELLER: I've got eight hundred from the man they call Alabama Sam, Mr. Sam Ellington.

RODNEY DENMAN: A thousand!

THE SLAVE AUCTION

SLAVE-SELLER: That's one thousand dollars
from Mr. Denman, who needs some help to
pick all that cotton he grows in the Mississippi
delta.

ELLINGTON: Twelve hundred!

DENMAN: Fifteen!

SLAVE-SELLER: I've got one thousand five
hundred dollars from Mr. Denman. One
thousand five hundred! *(Looks at Ellington.)*
Do I hear two thousand? *(Ellington shakes his
head.)* Seventeen fifty? *(Ellington shakes his
head again.)*

ELLINGTON: *(To Jeffrey.)* I'm sorry, boy, but I
don't have the money to buy her.

JEFFREY: But me and Dorcas, we supposed
to be married. We supposed to be together.
*(Ellington moves away as tears stream down
Jeffrey's face.)*

SLAVE-SELLER: I've got one thousand five
hundred dollars going once! Going twice!

Going three times! Sold! (*Bang!*) To Mr.
Rodney Denman of Ruleville, Mississippi!

*(There is the loud crack of lightning followed by
thunder so loud that the barn shakes for an instant
and the rain comes down harder than it has all
morning. However, even as loud as the rain is, the
painful sobbing of Jeffrey and Dorcas can still be
heard.)*

Interlude V

jeffrey

(Some years later after the slaves have been freed.
He sits beside a river.)

My new master was sorry he didn't buy Dorcas, 'cause I
ran away every chance I got. I was determined to get to
Mississippi and find Dorcas. But Master Ellington, he
catch me every time. After a while it was almost like a
game we played. He tried beating me to make me stop, but
wasn't nothing gon' keep me from trying to find Dorcas.
He say he was sorry he hadn't bought her, 'cause he spent
twice what she would've cost chasing after me. He say I
love Dorcas so much he would've thought I was a white
man. I don't know nothing about that. All I know is I had
to be with her or I was going to die.

The war what freed the slaves came. After it was over, the roads was filled with ex-slaves going this way and that looking for family members what had been sold away—husbands looking for wives and wives for husbands, men and women looking for children and children looking for their parents. Somebody would stop you on a road wanting to know where you were coming from and what your master's name was and did you know Lizzie or Peter or Vessie. One time I knew the person someone was looking for and that did wonderful things for my heart when I knew I'd helped two people find each other after slavery had split them apart.

I was trying to get to Mississippi and people point me in the direction. Once I got there I asked colored people where a place called Ruleville was. In Ruleville it was real easy to find Master Denman's place 'cause he had one of the biggest and most well-known plantations in the state.

I went there and I saw her before she saw me. She was sitting on the porch of a little cabin down in the slave quarters, or what used to be. She was sitting on the porch nursing a tiny baby. Then two children came out of the house. It was hard for me to believe what I was seeing. I couldn't believe that Dorcas hadn't waited for me. But maybe that wasn't Dorcas but somebody who looked like her.

As I walked toward the cabin she looked up. Her mouth dropped open and she got up slowly from the chair, still holding the baby.

"Jeffrey?" she say.

"Dorcas?" I say back.

She started crying in heavy sobs. "I didn't think I'd ever see you again," she say.

We just stand there looking at each other. She was even prettier than I remembered.

"I always knew I would find you," I say. "That's what kept me going for all these years."

She started crying real loud and the children look at her real worried-like. "Oh, Jeffrey! I am so sorry! I didn't think I'd ever see you again."

"Well, here I am and I still love you more than I love my own life. Will you come with me?"

"Oh, Jeffrey. I am sorry, but I got a husband. These are our children."

The tears were streaming down her face like rain on a window.

"Do you love your husband?" I ask.

"Not like I love you, but he's my husband, Jeffrey. He's a good provider and a good man."

"So am I." I'd been trying to hold my tears back, but I couldn't stop them no more and I started crying. "Can't nobody love you the way I do."

"Don't, Jeffrey. Please don't. I'm sorry."

And she turned around and hurried in the house, her children following her.

I stood there for the longest time. It was so quiet and still, like the world had come to an end. I don't know how long I stood there, but toward evening the hands started coming in from the field. A man walks up to me. He wanted to know if he could help me, if there was somebody I was looking for. I thanked him, but told him I'd found who I was looking for and I'd be going now. He invited me in, but I told him I was going. He went on into the house where Dorcas was and I turned and left.

I didn't know what to do or where to go so I've been walking the roads like so many others who were given their freedom but don't know how to practice it. I gained the freedom to go look for Dorcas. I was better off when I was a slave and could hold Dorcas in my mind.

Now I have nothing. I hope the Lord will forgive me for what I'm about to do and will have mercy on my soul. All I want is the peace in death which escaped me in life.

6

The Auctioning of Slaves Continues

Number 347—Tom, age 22; cotton hand

Sold for $1,260

Number 348—Judge Will, age 55; rice hand

Sold for $325

Number 349—Lowden, age 54; cotton hand

Number 350—Hagar, age 50; cotton hand

Number 351—Lowden, age 15; cotton, prime boy

Number 352—Silas, age 13; cotton, prime boy

Number 353—Lettia, age 11; cotton, prime girl

Sold for $300 each

Number 354—Fielding, age 21; cotton,
prime young man

Number 355—Abel, age 19; cotton,
prime young man

Sold for $1295 each

Number 356—Smith's Bill, aged; sore leg

Number 357—Leah, age 46; cotton hand

Number 358—Sally, age 9

Withdrawn

Number 359—Adam, age 24; prime man

Number 360—Charlotte, age 22; rice, prime woman

Number 361—Lesh, age 1

Sold for $570 each

Number 362—Maria, age 47; rice hand

Number 363—Luna, age 22; rice, prime woman

*Number 364—Clementina, age 17; rice, prime young
woman*

Sold for $950 each

Number 365—Tom, age 48; rice hand

Number 366—Harriet, age 41; rice hand

*Number 367—Wanney, age 19; rice hand, prime
young man*

Number 368—Deborah, age 6

Number 369—Infant, 3 months

Sold for $700 each

emma

The selling is coming to an end. I see Joe. I don't remember him being sold and I'm sorry. He is standing with the lady in the long blue dress who was looking at him before the selling started. I guess she's the one what bought him. She looks like a nice lady. I hope he'll be all right with her.

will

(*Enters the barn.*) After yesterday I didn't want to stay inside and watch the selling, so I stayed outside. There's a shed next to the blacksmith's shop where I could stay out of the rain and talk with the other slaves who came here with their masters.

All I want to do now is find Master and find out what he want me to do. I'd like nothing better than to go back to the plantation, sit in the kitchen by the stove and let the heat dry these wet clothes and have Mattie make me a cup of elderberry tea.

I'm glad of one thing, though. This rain is finally letting up.

(His eyes roam quickly around the barn as he looks for his master. He sees Emma at the far end of the barn, Sarah holding her hand. Will looks confused, unable to understand why she is there. He sees the slave-seller talking with a woman in a long blue dress. He sees the slave-seller point in Emma's direction, then watches as the slave-seller and the woman in the long blue dress make their way across the barn to where Master Butler stands in a corner.)

emma

The lady in the long blue dress and slave-seller were looking in this direction. Ain't nothing over here for them to see. Now the slave-seller say something to Master and then Master and the lady start talking. Master shakes his head. She talks some more. Master don't shake his head this time. She talk some more. This time Master nods slowly. The woman holds out her hand and Master shakes it. The woman turn around and look over here again. Miss Frances is looking over this way, too. Master look like he found something very interesting on the floor to stare at. Master say something to Frances and she starts in this direction.

I see Papa. He's staring at Master and looks angry about something.

FRANCES: *(Calls out loudly as she comes near.)* Sarah! Papa wants you!

SARAH: *(Starts toward her sister, still holding Emma's hand.)* Come on, Emma. It's time to go home.

FRANCES: *(Close enough to Sarah and Emma that she doesn't have to raise her voice.)* Emma can't come.

SARAH: Why not?

FRANCES: Because.

SARAH: Where you going, Emma?

FRANCES: *(Takes Sarah's hand and begins to pull on her.)* Come on, Sarah. We've got to go! Come on, now! Papa's going to get angry if you don't come right now!

EMMA: What's going on, Miss Frances? What was the lady in the blue dress talking to your papa about?

FRANCES: Papa said I shouldn't say anything to you.

EMMA: *(Beginning to understand what she just witnessed.)* Frances? Did Master Butler sell me to that lady? Is that what they was shaking hands about?

FRANCES: *(Refuses to look at Emma.)* Come on, Sarah! Now! *(Her voice is strident and she is on the verge of tears.)* Please, Sarah! Papa wants you to come with me!

SARAH: Emma? Papa wouldn't sell you. I know he wouldn't do that.

EMMA: *(Puts her arms around Sarah and holds her tightly, blinking her eyes rapidly to hold back her own tears.)* You go on with your sister. Your papa wants you. You go on now.

SARAH: But, what about you? I want you to come.

EMMA: You go on. Everything will be all right. *(Takes her arms from around Sarah, looks at Frances and opens her arms. Frances runs to Emma's embrace, tears trickling down her face. The two hug tightly. After a moment, Emma releases her.)* You go on now. You don't want to keep your papa waiting. *(The two girls walk slowly away, holding each other's hands, as Mistress Henfield walks toward Emma.)*

MASTER: *(When the girls reach him he reaches down and hits Sarah hard on her behind.)* When I say for you to come, I mean for you to come right now! You hear me! Don't you be looking at Emma like you need her permission to do what I say! *(He hits her again, harder. Sarah starts screaming and runs back toward Emma. Master runs and picks her up. She starts kicking at him.)*

WILL: *(Looks at Master Butler trying to control Sarah, who is squirming and kicking so hard that he is forced to put her down. Sarah runs toward Emma again, and again, her father catches her. Will sees the woman in the long blue dress going toward Emma. He knows immediately what has transpired and hurries to Master Butler.)* No! No! Master, you promised! You promised! You promised!

MASTER: *(To Will.)* Take Sarah out to the coach and stay with her.

WILL: How could you do this? We grew up together. We was like brothers! How could you do this?

MASTER: But we aren't brothers, Will! Now, take Sarah out to the coach or Mattie won't see *you* this evening, either.

WILL: I should have let you drown. *(Reaches down and picks up Sarah, whose cries diminish in his arms. Leaves, holding Sarah tightly as she holds him tightly around the neck.)*

(At the opposite side of the barn.)

MISTRESS HENFIELD: Master Butler tells me your name is Emma and that you are very good at taking care of children. Is that so?

EMMA: *(Her eyes are down. She does not want anyone to see her face. Not yet. Not yet. Not until her face is as plain as a board. Not until she looks like she is not here.)* Yes, ma'am.

MISTRESS HENFIELD: I have a little girl who's almost two. Do you think you can take care of someone that little?

EMMA: Yes, ma'am.

MISTRESS HENFIELD: Have you ever heard of Kentucky?

EMMA: No, ma'am.

MISTRESS HENFIELD: We live in Kentucky, which is a long way from Georgia.

EMMA: Yes, ma'am.

MISTRESS HENFIELD: I am Mistress Henfield.

EMMA: Yes, ma'am.

MISTRESS HENFIELD: Well, we should get started. You don't have anything to bring with you, of course. Come, child. My little girl, Ruth, is outside in the coach with Sampson. Master Butler drove a hard bargain for you. I hope you're worth all I paid, Emma. You go stand in that line. Master Butler has a little good-bye present for all his slaves.

EMMA: Yes, ma'am.

emma

I don't know what to feel. I want to scream. I want to cry. And at the same time I feel like my heart has stopped beating and I will never feel anything again. At least the other slaves knew what was going to happen to them. They had time to say good-bye, but my mama is at the plantation expecting me to come back and help her prepare the supper and serve the table tonight. She don't know she ain't never going to see me again.

Mistress Henfield is taking me across the barn to where the other slaves are standing as if they are waiting for something. She acts like I don't have feelings, like it don't hurt me in my heart to be sold to her like I was nothing more than a bag of walnuts or sack of onions. How would she feel if one minute she was talking to her daughter and the next minute somebody took her away? She don't think about that. She treat me like I ain't no more than a box to be picked up and moved wherever she want it to go. She seems to be a nice lady, but she don't know how much I hate her, how much I'll always hate her.

THE AUCTIONING OF SLAVES CONTINUES

I'm standing in the line of slaves and see Joe a few people ahead of me. I call out to him. He turns and looks surprised to see me and comes back to where I am.

JOE: Emma? What you doing here? Master Butler sell you?

EMMA: That's what he did. Sold me to the lady I think bought you.

JOE: Mistress Henfield?

EMMA: The one in the long blue dress.

JOE: That's Mistress Henfield. I'm sorry you got sold, but I'm glad we gon' be together.

EMMA: Me, too. What we standing in this line for?

JOE: Master Butler is giving each one of us a silver dollar.

EMMA: He think that going to make us feel better?

JOE: A lot of these niggers think this shows what

a good master he is. It's the first real money they've ever had in their hands.

EMMA: Don't matter.

JOE: No, it don't. *(He grasps Emma's hand and she holds his in return.)* We the closest each other got to family now, Emma. That's more important than anything.

emma

He's right. Sometimes family ain't blood but them what are by your side when you need somebody. The line is getting shorter and shorter. Now it's our turn. Master is standing there with a silly grin on his face, holding that dollar out, but Joe walks on past him like he ain't even there.

Now it's my turn. I stop and look at Master, look him straight in the eye. He starts blinking his eyes real fast like he wishes he was a bird and his eyelids was wings and he could fly away. I keep staring at him until he starts to get real red in the face. Then I walk on.

As I step out of the barn I am surprised to see that the rain has stopped and that the sun is shining brightly through a large hole in the clouds. I can feel its warmth on my arms and face.

SARAH: *(Looking out of the coach, sees Emma.)* Emma! Emma! *(She opens the coach door and runs out and throws herself into Emma's arms. Will follows right behind her. He hugs Emma with Sarah between them. Emma can no longer hold back her tears and she begins to cry.)*

WILL: Don't cry, child. You got to be strong now. You hear me? Strong! *(To Joe.)* You be strong, too. Emma ain't got nobody now but you. You hear that? You understand what I'm saying?

JOE: Yes, suh. I understand. I'll take good care of her.

EMMA: *(She hugs her father tighter.)* Tell Mama I won't forget nothing she taught me. Tell

her I'll be all right. And I'll be strong, Papa.
I'll be strong!

emma

When Papa and I take our arms from around each
other I can feel his tears on the side of my face,
and the front of my dress is wet with Sarah's tears.
The lady in the blue dress—Mistress Henfield—is
coming toward us and quickly I kiss Papa and then
I kiss Sarah and give her another hug.

EMMA: *(To Sarah.)* You reminds me so much of
   your mama. You think you can have a good
   heart like your mama does? You think you can
   do that? *(Sarah nods her head several times and
   then hugs Emma tightly until Emma takes the girl's
   arms from around her waist.)*

emma

Mistress Henfield comes. Joe and I follow her

across the driveway to where her coach is. I sit
inside with her and a little girl. Joe sits outside,
next to the slave driving the coach. The coach
starts to move. I put my head out the window
and see Papa and Sarah standing in the driveway,
waving. I wave back. I keep looking at them.
They get smaller and smaller. When the coach
goes around a bend in the road they disappear.

Interlude VI

sampson

*(Driving the coach carrying Emma and Joe
to their new home in Kentucky.)*

*The boy sits on the seat beside me, shivering like it's the
middle of winter. He scared. He's probably feeling like a
leaf that got blown off a tree and don't know where it's
going to land.*

"Everything's going to be all right, son. Mistress
Henfield, she a good woman. She's a widow lady. Her
husband died a while back and left her to run the plantation by herself. It's not a big place, not like what I
understand you used to. There's just a few of us niggers
on the place and Mistress Henfield treat us almost like
family. We have our own gardens. She lets us hire out our

time in town. I work for the blacksmith and earn some hard cash money. Mistress takes some of it, of course, but the rest I get to keep for myself. You feel bad now because of all you leaving behind, but when you see where you're going, you'll be happy Mistress Henfield bought you."

The boy don't say nothing for the longest time. Then, I hear this voice that don't have nothing but hate in it. "If that's all you got to say, old man, then you can stop talking."

It's all I can do to keep from pushing this boy off the coach. Mistress be better off if I left him lying in the road. I'm trying to make him feel better, trying to be his friend, but he talk to me like he thinks I'm a fool. He's the fool. He don't understand that slavery's the best thing ever happened to us niggers. Where would we be if we didn't have the white folks to take care of us? We'd be out there in the woods or on the road somewhere begging for our supper. I don't have to worry about getting a good meal every day or having a roof over my head. And I'll have that every day of my life if I do what the white folks tell me.

7

The Kitchen

(The kitchen of Pierce Butler's house. It is night. From the dining room comes sounds of people talking loudly and laughing. Mattie stands at the stove, cooking. In a corner of the kitchen Sarah is asleep at a table, using her folded arms as a pillow for her head.)

mattie

I knew something terrible had happened the minute I heard that girl screaming. From way down the road I could hear her, and the closer they got, the louder her screaming was. I ran outside and the coach had hardly stopped before she was out the door and running to me.

"Papa sold Emma! Papa sold Emma!" she sobbed.

Master Butler got out of the coach and he couldn't even look at me. He picked Frances up like he was afraid she was going to run to me, too, and went in the house like he didn't know I was standing there.

Will was sitting atop the coach and the tears were just flowing down his face. That's the first time I've ever seen that man cry. He didn't even cry when his parents died. "At least they not in slavery no more," was all he said about that.

He got down from the coach and come over to where I was outside the door to the kitchen and he hugged me real hard and kept saying over and over, "I'm sorry, Mattie. I'm sorry," like it was his fault. Sarah was there in between us like she wanted as much of the hugging as she could get, and Will picked her up. She put one arm around my neck and one around Will's and the three of us had ourselves a good cry.

Master must've been watching from inside the house, 'cause the next thing I know he was on the porch calling for Sarah.

"You come here right now, Sarah, or I'll spank your little bottom again!"

Sarah hopped out of Will's arms and scurried behind the two of us as if there was something we could do to protect her. And maybe we did, because I stared at Master, looked him in the eye with the purest and holiest anger I have ever felt. Seem like it was more than Master could take and he went on back in the house.

Will had to go put the wagon away and brush and feed the mules. I had to finish getting the food ready for Master's banquet celebrating all the money he made from selling his slaves.

"You should go on in the house to your papa now, Miss Sarah," I said to her.

She shook her head vigorously. "I hate him! I hate him!"

"Don't you be saying something like that around me, young lady! He's your father. You don't be hating your father."

"But I do, Mattie. I do!"

I couldn't argue with her, not as much hatred as I was feeling in my heart for that man. I didn't know I had so much hatred in me. If my hatred was fire, wouldn't nothing be left standing on this place.

Miss Sarah followed me back to the kitchen. I made a cup of mint tea and gave it to her. She drank a little bit, put her arms on the table, laid her head down and promptly fell asleep. The poor thing had worn herself out crying. But every now and then I hear her whimper and moan in her sleep.

Whatever time I get to bed tonight I know I'm not going to sleep. I didn't know a person could be angry and sorrowful at the same time, but that's what I am. When I think about Master I get so angry I think I can hear my blood boiling like hot water in a tea kettle. But then, I start thinking about Emma and tears rush to my eyes. Will said the lady what bought her lives in Kentucky.

I wish I knew how far that is from Georgia. Will said it's quite a ways. Said it'll take almost a week for Emma to get there.

Lord, please have mercy on my child! Please, I beg you. Have mercy on my child!

MASTER: *(Puts his head inside kitchen door.)* How long before you'll be ready to start serving, Mattie?

MATTIE: Everything's about ready now.

MASTER: *(Master looks at Mattie with sorrow in his eyes. Seeing the hatred on Mattie's face he now regrets having sold Emma. He opens his mouth as if to speak, closes it, and finally speaks softly, haltingly.)* Mattie? I—I don't quite know what to say. I don't know what got into me.

MATTIE: I don't know you anymore. You look like Master Pierce Butler, but you don't act like him. If you was the Master Butler I know, then you would have remembered that my black mother nursed you and me at the same time. The Master Butler I know got his nourishment in the milk from a black mother's breasts. You, me, and Will grew up here together like sister and brother. You look like Master Butler, but that's about all you got in common with the Master Butler I know.

MASTER: Mattie, I know how it seems, but you have to understand—

MATTIE: All I understand is that my only child is on her way to some place called Kentucky and I ain't never gon' see her again. What you want me to understand beyond that? I hope you burn in hell! *(Pierce Butler gives Mattie a look of disgust, shuts the door and returns to his guests.)*

That's right, Master. Run away! I ain't got no respect for a man who does wrong and won't own up to it. Run all you want, Master. God knows and I know: you done wrong this day and Satan is going to put you on the fire like you was pork ribs at a barbecue. *(As Mattie spoons mashed potatoes from a pot into a serving bowl, she spits into the potatoes several times, then stirs them again. She spits into the gravy and stirs. Spit, stir. Spit, stir. Then, with a smile on her face, she begins carrying the food into the dining room.)*

will

After I take care of the mules I wash up and change into the clothes I have to wear when Master has a big dinner like tonight and Mattie needs somebody to help serve at the table.

Every white person at the table knows what happened today, knows that my heart is so full of grief that I'm afraid it's going to bust wide open. But they expect me to bow and grin and say, "Yassuh," and "No, ma'am." And I do. I hate myself for doing it, but I can't seem to help it. It's the way I been trained. And if I don't pretend to be happy and bow and grin, well, no telling what Master might do, since I never thought he'd be so mean as to sell Emma. He could sell me to somebody sitting at that table and Mattie would lose her whole family in one day.

Master want to pretend like me and Mattie don't have feelings same as him. He don't want to see the grief weighing us down like we carrying mules on our shoulders. This grief will never end even if I was to live as long as a star in the sky. Well, I'm gon' make Master sorry for giving me this grief.

I'm going to talk to Uncle Isaac. He's a Guinea nigger, pure African. He talk about coming across on a big ship long, long time ago. He can work all kinds of spells. He takes parts of different kinds of animals and puts them together with something that belongs to the person you want to put a spell on, and then he say a lot of words in African and that's it! I'm gon' take him some of the hair from Master's comb and brush and see if he can't do a death spell. I got a feeling that after all this selling, Uncle Isaac might be glad to make one for Master Butler.

(Late night. All the guests have left. Mattie and Will are in the kitchen cleaning up. Sarah still sleeps at the table.)

MASTER: *(Enters kitchen without looking at Mattie and Will. Goes over to table where Sarah still sleeps.)* Sarah? Honey? It's time to come upstairs and go to bed.

SARAH: *(Awakes slowly and looks up at her father through sleepy eyes. Then, as she recognizes who it is, she is suddenly alert.)* I hate you! I hate you!

MASTER: You shouldn't say something like that to your father. Come upstairs. It's time for bed.

SARAH: I'm going to sleep with Mattie and Will tonight.

(Mattie and Will exchange astonished glances.)

MASTER: *(Angrily to Mattie and Will.)* Which one
of you put that idea in her head?

MATTIE: Maybe she don't want to sleep here
because you went and sold away the person that
was like a mama to her. *(To Sarah.)* Honey, I
don't think you'd get a good night's sleep in the
quarters. Our bed's not near as nice as yours.

SARAH: I don't care. I don't want to stay here
tonight. *(To her father.)* I don't want to sleep
upstairs and you can't make me!

MASTER: Do you want me to go upstairs and
get my razor strop? I'll beat you so hard you
won't be able to sit down for a week!

SARAH: Mother was right. She said if she'd
known how mean you were she would have
never married you.

MASTER: *(He is stung by his daughter's words and
flushes red with anger.)* Well, it's pretty clear that

you are your mother's child and not mine. If you want to spend the night in the slave quarters with niggers, you go right ahead. That sounds like something your mother would've done, if I'd let her.

Interlude VII

sarah as a young woman

I felt so proud when he said I was Mama's child and not his. I wished Emma had been there to hear him say that about me. I don't know if I would've known how to react to her being sold if Emma's last words to me hadn't been to tell me to have as good a heart as my mama's.

When I was sitting there at the table in the kitchen I wasn't asleep as much of the time as Mattie thought. I suppose I slept some, but most of the time I was thinking about how to have a good heart. Mama cared about the slaves and she never called them by that awful word, not even behind their backs. So, I decided having a good heart meant staying with Will and Mattie. They had just lost their daughter, and in my childish mind I suppose I thought I could be Emma, if only for a night or two.

Of course, being a mother now, I realize how foolish that was. If I were to lose my Emma, someone else's child couldn't fill that place in my heart. No, looking back on it now, I understand that I needed them that night far more than they needed me.

I stayed that night and I missed my bed and my room and I agreed to go back the next night only if Mattie stayed with me until I went to sleep. And she did. It was almost like having Emma there.

Papa thought things would be different once we went to Philadelphia. He thought I would forget. But I didn't, and I was hurt that he didn't want to remember. I thought about Emma every day and that's not an exaggeration. I still do. At night I would look up at the stars and find the Big Dipper and wonder if Emma was looking up right at that moment and seeing it too.

I thought I hated Papa, but as he was dying, I realized I didn't. Hatred is as much of a relationship as love. I almost wished I had hated him, because what I felt was far, far worse. I had no respect for him as a man, no respect for how he had lived his life. Yes, he was my father and I honored him because he had helped to give me life. More than that I could not do.

I sat there by his bed and he so desperately wanted to hear me say that I loved him. "Do you love your papa, Sarah?" he asked, his voice so weak I could barely hear him.

All I had to do was nod my head. I didn't even have to say anything. Just a simple nod and he would've died happy. But I wanted him to feel what Mattie and Will felt when he sold Emma.

He looked at me, his eyes pleading. I took his hand in mine and patted it lightly and then left the room. Frances hurried in and I heard her burst into a sob. Between the time I left and she entered, he died.

I cried.

8

The Henfield Plantation

(A year later. The Henfield place in Kentucky. Emma and Joe are in the kitchen of Mistress Henfield's house, cleaning up after dinner.)

emma

I look forward to this part of the day. When Joe finishes brushing down the horses and the mules and giving them their feed, he comes here and helps me clean up after I've served Mistress her supper. I always save him something to eat and we sit around the table and talk about things, like Mama and Papa did.

Since Sampson been sick, Joe drives Mistress to town when she needs to go. That led to him getting a job in town working at the general store a couple of days a week. But he always gets back in time for us to have our supper together in the kitchen and to help me clean up. I like having someone I can talk to, somebody who listens to me and understands what I'm saying.

EMMA: *(To Joe.)* Mistress Henfield keeps asking me if it's better for me here than when I was on the Butler plantation. I tell her what she want to hear. There ain't near as much work to do. There ain't nobody to cook for except her and Miss Ruth. Taking care of Miss Ruth ain't near as much work as looking after Miss Sarah and Miss Frances was. But that don't mean it's better being here. It would be better if I could be with my mama and papa.

   If you weren't here, Joe, I don't know what I would do. It's nice being with somebody who remembers the same things I do. I like it when we laugh together over some of the stories that Junius used to tell and you hum some of the tunes that Ezekiel used to play on his fiddle. What I like most, though, is when we talk about the things we remember about my mama and papa and yours. They don't seem so far away then.

JOE: You know I was always sweet on you. And I think you're sweet on me. Don't you think it's time we jumped the broom?

EMMA: Joe, you know how I feel about that. If we jump the broom, then the next thing we be having children and you know I don't want to have a child and take care of her and have her grow up, and then one day she be sold away from me. I can't have no child what's going to be a slave. I just can't do it!

JOE: *(Lowers his voice.)* What if we don't have to be slaves no more?

EMMA: We gon' be slaves until the day they throw us in a hole in the ground.

JOE: Maybe not. *(Lowers his voice to almost a*

whisper.) Yesterday at the store things were pretty quiet. Wasn't much to do and wasn't nobody there. Me and Mr. Henry was sitting around the potbellied stove in the center of the store and he say real quiet to me, "Joe? You ever think about being free?"

I like to have almost fell off the chair. I never had a white person ask me about being free. I wondered if he was trying to get me in trouble. What if I said that's all I think about? Would he tell Mistress? She's a nice lady and all, but as nice as she is, she don't want no slave on her place to be thinking about freedom.

So when Mr. Henry ask me, I don't know what to say. He surprised me even more when he said, "I apologize. I shouldn't have asked you that. You don't know me. Why should you tell me or any white man the truth? So, let's just leave it like this. I don't know if you know it, but this town ain't far from the Ohio River.

On this side of the river there are slaves. But on the other side there ain't no slaves. And I know some people over there, people who want to help slaves on this side get across the river to where they don't have to be slaves no more."

And he don't say nothing else. I sat there not knowing what to do. One part of me wanted to jump up and shout and holler, *Mr. Henry, get me across that river now!* But another part of me was scared. What if he wasn't telling the truth? What if he was trying to trap me and instead of being free, I'd end up being sold again, sold far away from you?

Then, today, wasn't nobody else in the store. Me and Mr. Henry was sitting by the stove again and he took three pieces of kindling wood. He laid one at an angle, and then the second one at an angle so that the two pieces met at the top. Then he took the third piece and laid it across the other two.

"Joe? I could be thrown in jail for what I'm about to do, but you see them three sticks I just laid out?"

I allowed as I did.

"That's the first letter of the alphabet. That's the letter *A*."

My eyes got big. Was he teaching me to read?

He went over behind the counter and come back with a empty croaker sack that had some writing on it. He handed it to me.

"You see anything on that sack look like them three sticks on the floor?"

I was holding the sack in my hands, but I was so excited my hands were trembling and I could barely see what was on the sack. But there it was! I saw it!

"Right here!" I said, pointing to the letter. "That's it, ain't it? Ain't that it?" I was so excited I could hardly stand it.

Mr. Henry smiled. "That's right, Joe. That's the letter *A*."

I ain't never had a grin on my face like I had at that minute. I could read. Leastways, I could make out one letter.

He say, "Don't you let on to nobody what I'm doing. It's against the law to teach a slave to read and I could be put in jail, or worse. This is just between you and me." *(Joe takes three knives and forms them into the letter A.)* That's what it looks like, Emma. That's the letter *A*!

EMMA: *(Stares at the letter for a long time.)* What did you say he say about us being free, Joe?

JOE: He say there's a big river called Ohio and on this side of the river, there's slaves. But on the other side, there ain't no slaves. And he say he knows some people who want to get slaves from this side of the river to the other.

EMMA: I heard Mistress talkin' once about the

Ohio River. It was one time when she had company. I didn't hear her say nothing about freedom being on the other side, but she mentioned the name of a place, a city that was on the other side of the river.

JOE: Mr. Henry said the name of a city, too. It was a funny sounding word. Cinci—Cinci—something.

EMMA: Cincinnati? Was that it?

JOE: That's it! Cincinnati! *(In their excitement their voices have gotten louder and each puts an index finger to their lips to signal that they need to be quiet.)*

EMMA: Joe, I believe Mr. Henry is telling you the truth. And I ain't never heard of no white man teaching a slave how to read. One of the biggest fights Master Butler and the mistress had was when she said she was gon' teach the slaves to read and write. A few days after that she was headed back to Philadelphia. Any white man who wants a slave to learn to read and write has a heart like Mistress Butler. That's a heart I trust.

JOE: If we make it to Cincinnati, will you be my wife?

EMMA: Joe, I'll not only be your wife, I'll have as many babies as you can give me. *(They embrace.)*

JOE: What shall we do about Charles?

EMMA: What about Charles?

JOE: I want to tell him and see if he wants to come with us.

EMMA: And what if he tell his papa? Sampson will run as fast as he can and tell Mistress.

JOE: Charles ain't like his papa. Since Sampson been sick, me and Charles talk a lot when we working in the barn. He hates slavery worse than we do.

EMMA: And what about Winnie and that baby they got?

JOE: That's how come he wants to be free. He say he don't want his baby growing up in no slavery. He don't want his son to grow up to be no slavery lover like Sampson.

EMMA: I don't know. We don't know what we gettin' ourselves into. If it was just Charles, maybe. But Winnie and the baby, too? I don't know, Joe.

JOE: Charles ain't gon' leave without Winnie and the baby.

EMMA: I don't like it, but I can see you got your heart set on bringing them along. I guess if I had a friend, I'd be wanting to bring her.

JOE: Thanks, Emma!

Interlude VIII

sampson

A while back one of the mules kicked me in the shin. Mistress sent for the doctor and he made a poultice for my leg. It's getting better, but I still have to lay here on my pallet for a while longer. But even if I can't go nowhere I know that nigger from Georgia and my boy, Charles, are up to something. Charles and that boy are taking care of the horses and the mules. A few nights ago Charles come in and he was happy about something. I asked him what he so happy about. He say, nothing, but ain't nobody happy for no reason.

So I lie here on my pallet and think: What could have happened that would make Charles so happy? After Charles told me that Mistress was having Joe drive her into town and that Joe was working a couple of afternoons at the store, I knew all I needed to know.

I know things about Mr. Henry. I do! One time a few years back, right after he come to town and opened that store, I had taken the mistress into town. Mr. Henry was helping me load up the wagon with supplies that Mistress had just bought. She'd gone off to take care of some business or other at the bank. I was in the back of the store with Mr. Henry and was about to pick up a fifty-pound sack of flour when Mr. Henry ask me, "Sampson? You ever think about being free?"

I looked at the man like he had lost his mind. I thought that man was trying to get me in trouble. If I said yes, he might go tell Mistress that I was dangerous because only dangerous niggers think about something like that. But I told him the truth.

"Naw, suh. From what I understand them free niggers up north wish they was in slavery because freedom is too hard for a nigger. Yes, suh. Mistress takes care of this nigger. Yes, suh. I don't have to worry about where I'm going to sleep at night. Don't have to worry if I'm going

to eat every day. If I get sick, Mistress send for the doctor and he come right away. What I want to be free for and have to worry about all them things myself?"

Mr. Henry didn't say nothing else, but ever since then I kept my distance from that man. I don't know what he was up to, but whatever it was, it meant trouble for this nigger. I reckon now I should've told Mistress about him. Don't know why I didn't. Maybe it's because I felt sorry for some of the niggers on Master Pendle's plantation. He treats his niggers hard, and if some of them had a chance to escape, I wouldn't stand in the way.

But Mistress Henfield treats us good and don't give us no reason to want to run away. But that Joe! I bet anything Mr. Henry got to talking about freedom to that boy and he ain't got no more sense than to listen. And then, Joe talked to Charles, who ain't got the sense he was born with.

I don't let on that I know something's up. I also don't let on that I'm getting better. I just lay here and pretend like I'm sleeping, but I'm just waiting. I don't know what I'm waiting for, but I'll know when it happens.

9

Charles and Sampson's Cabin

(Charles lies on a pallet on one side of the small log cabin next to his sleeping wife and baby. On the other side of the room his father, Sampson, lies on his pallet. Both are awake but neither knows the other is. Each is alone with his thoughts. Outside there is the faint sound of distant thunder.)

charles

I'm scared. Ever since I can remember, I done thought about getting away from here, about being free. But now that I've got the chance, I don't know what to do. Papa has always made being free sound like the worst thing there is. He say freedom don't mean nothing but worry—worry about how to get something to eat and some place to stay and how to pay for the doctor and all like that. I suppose he's right, but I don't think that's all there is to being free.

What about how a person feels in his heart? And I just know my heart would feel a lot better if Mistress Henfield didn't own me like she own her house and the mules and horses in her barn. She can sell me away from Winnie tomorrow and I couldn't say a word about it. Being free is knowing that me and Winnie can be together the rest of our lives and can't nobody say different.

But still, I'm scared. I don't know what's worse— staying here and being owned by Mistress Henfield and hoping she didn't sell me away from Winnie or Winnie away from me; or going with Joe and Emma and trying to get across the river, not knowing where we're going and or what we'll do?

I'm ashamed of myself. I guess I got some of my papa in me. I don't love Mistress Henfield the way he do and I don't grin and bow around white folks the way he do. When I'm around Joe I talk like I'm a lot braver than I really am, but deep down, I like not having to worry about all the things I'd have to worry about if I was free. And maybe that's reason enough to get away from here. A real man don't live his life letting somebody else take care of him like he was their child. Mistress Henfield treats all us niggers like we are pet dogs that sit when she say sit, fetch when she say fetch, and stand up on our hind legs and beg when she say so.

If I stay here I'm afraid I ain't gon' end up no better than my papa. I don't want my daughter to look at me the way I look at him. That would hurt my heart worse than anything in the world. Better to try and get to freedom than stay here.

I just wish I wasn't so scared.

sampson

I ain't never told him and I should. I know I should. But I can't. He hates me now, but what if he knew the truth?

I was a different kind of person when I was his age. Wasn't no slave on no plantation anywhere what hated slavery more than me. This was down in Alabama, where they got some of the meanest slave owners in this country. Slavery is so bad on some of the plantations down there that the niggers don't pray for freedom; they pray for death. If they was free they'd still have to live with the memories of all the things they'd seen, all the things that had been done to them. Death was the only thing that would give them peace.

The plantation I was on was one of the worst. The overseer would put the lash on you if he thought you were thinking something he didn't want you to think. First time he put the lash on me I was working in the fields. Don't know what I did or what he thought I did. I was putting cottonseed in the ground. Next thing I knew—*pow!* My back was burning up with pain and it was wet.

I knew that was blood, mine. He turned his horse around and went on back to the end of the row. To this day I don't know why he struck me with the whip. But I didn't need no reason. I wanted to kill him with my bare hands and I knew I would if I had to look at that white, pasty face the next morning. So that night I ran away.

I'd overheard one of the old slaves say that you could be free if you followed the North Star. So that's what I tried to do. That meant I could only travel at night, which was the scariest time to be out and about. I didn't have nothing to eat and it was early spring, which meant that there weren't any berries or anything like that to eat in the woods.

I don't know what happened. I guess I just ended up walking around and around in a circle, because the third day after I escaped, I found myself back in the woods at the edge of the planta-tion. I was tired; I was hungry; I needed water. I guess I just gave up. I came staggering out of the woods at the far end of the field. The ol' overseer saw me and he came galloping over on that big black horse of his and he took the whip to me right there. *Pow!* That whip wrapped itself around my body tight. The overseer pulled on it and it got a little tighter. I stumbled and the overseer started dragging me behind the horse. I guess I fainted, because the next thing I remember is being tied by my wrists to a tree limb on that big oak that sat in the master's front yard.

The overseer whupped me until his arm was so tired he couldn't hold it up anymore. But I had fainted long before that. He left me hanging in the tree and I might be hanging there still if not for Master Henfield. He was visiting my master and when he saw me hanging by my wrists from that tree, he took pity on me. I never did get the story of how it went, but next thing I knew I was being cut down from the tree.

Master Henfield was there looking down at me. He say, "Boy, your master say you a troublemaker, somebody what like to run away."

I could barely keep my eyes open, but I knowed this was probably my one and only chance. I told him, "No, suh. I run away 'cause the overseer whupped me for no reason. That's why I run away. I'm a good nigger, massuh. Yes, suh. Sampson is the best nigger there is."

A few days after that, when I was well enough to travel, Master Henfield brought me here, and here I've been ever since.

What Charles don't understand is that you can live better in slavery than you can when you free, if you know how to treat white folks. As long as they think you got about as much sense as a rock, and you tell them how good they is, they'll do almost anything you want them to do. Mistress Henfield think she own, me but I'm the one what own her.

My boy don't seem to understand that. I got to stay alert because he's likely to do something that will ruin everything for me. And I done worked too hard and too long to let some young fool ruin things for me.

10

The Henfield Plantation Barn

(It is late at night. Emma and Joe are in the plantation barn. Outside lightning flashes across the sky followed by deep rumbles of thunder.)

EMMA: I got a bad feeling, Joe.

JOE: You just scared. That's all. Everything's gon' be all right. Just think, Emma! This time tomorrow we gon' be free.

EMMA: I hope you right. Where's Charles and Winnie? What's taking them so long? Maybe we should leave without 'em.

JOE: Don't worry. They be here. They probably had to wait until Sampson fell asleep. *(Just then the door to the stable opens and Charles enters quickly, followed by Winnie, holding a baby.)* See! Here they are!

CHARLES: Sorry. I waited until I heard Papa snoring real loud.

(Emma goes and hugs Winnie and looks at the baby.)

WINNIE: I fed him real good. He should sleep for a long time. Leastways I hope he does. He's been real colicky of late.

JOE: Well, we best be on our way if we going.

(The barn door opens again and Sampson walks in, holding a lamp.)

SAMPSON: I'm afraid you not going anywhere, boy, except on the auction block.

CHARLES: Papa! What're you doing here?

SAMPSON: Trying to save you!

CHARLES: I thought you were 'sleep.

SAMPSON: You thought what I wanted you to think. I knowed you was up to something and when you left tonight with Winnie and my grandbaby I knowed there was only one thing you could be doing if you was taking them with you.

I can understand these two getting a crazy idea in their head. But you, son! Mistress been good to us. Why you want to hurt her like this? I thought I taught you better than this. You supposed to be grateful for all she done for us.

CHARLES: And what exactly has she done that I'm supposed to thank her for? You say she's a nice lady, Papa. And if what you mean by *nice* is that she don't beat us, then you right. She's nice. But she ain't nice enough to set us free.

SAMPSON: Free! What you know about being free? Freedom ain't all you think it is.

CHARLES: I'll never know unless I try it for myself. Joe? Emma? Winnie? Let's go. Time's a-wasting. *(Charles starts to move toward the door.*

Sampson blocks his path. Charles tries to step around his father and Sampson moves to block his path again.) Papa? Don't do this, please. Just step aside and let us pass.

JOE: I'm sorry, Charles. It ain't that simple.

CHARLES: What do you mean?

JOE: If we let him just step aside, he'll run and tell Mistress Henfield and we'll be caught before we off the plantation.

CHARLES: You're right, Joe. I'm sorry, Papa. I'm real sorry. *(Charles hits his father in the stomach and as Sampson bends over from the power of the blow, Charles hits him on the chin, knocking him down. The lamp drops from Sampson's hand and onto the floor of the barn, which is covered with straw. Tears stream down Charles' face.)*

Please forgive me, Papa. Please forgive me.

(As they hurry out of the barn and into the darkness, rain starts to fall. Charles sees smoke coming from

beneath the barn door. He starts to go back, but Joe grabs his arm.)

JOE: We got to go! Now!
CHARLES: Papa! Papa!

(Joe pulls him and they disappear into the darkness.)

Interlude IX

mistress henfield as an old woman

That night was the beginning of the end. I was awakened by the sound of the horses whinnying and the mules braying. I looked out the window and saw flames coming from the barn.

Thank God it was raining. If it hadn't been I would've lost the whole barn and all the horses and mules. I ran outside and started hollering for help and the slaves came and got the horses and mules out. That was when they found Sampson lying on the barn floor, moaning. He'd obviously been the first one to notice the barn was burning and had gone to get the horses and mules out but had been overcome by smoke. Thank God they were able to drag him out, but he hasn't been the same since.

In all the excitement I had clean forgotten about Ruth. What if she had woken up and I wasn't there? I looked around at the slaves who stood mutely watching the fire. I didn't see Emma among them, but of course not. Emma's first thought would have been of Ruth and she would have gone to her.

But I hurried back to the house to be sure. The minute I stepped inside I heard Ruth screaming at the top of her lungs. I ran upstairs and she was standing in the doorway to my room, alone.

I was disappointed in Emma and if it hadn't been raining so hard I would've gone to the slave quarters that night and reprimanded her for not having understood that her first thought should have been my daughter's well-being.

The next morning I understood everything, of course, when I was awakened by Ruth's crying and calling for Emma. I went in and got Ruth. When I got downstairs everything was quiet. I went in the kitchen still expecting to see Emma at the stove and Joe standing by the hearth, drinking coffee. The kitchen was empty.

I felt like such a fool. I felt even more the fool when I went to the slave quarters to tell Charles and Winnie that they were going to have to work in the house now. But the cabin they'd shared with Sampson was empty.

To this day I don't understand how they could have betrayed me like that. I wasn't mean to them. They ate well. I even let them earn a little money for themselves, and every slave had his own vegetable garden. And this was the thanks I got.

Well, I wasn't going to wait around for the rest of the niggers to run away. And I couldn't trust that they wouldn't. I sold every last one of them, sold them to Jake Pendle, who didn't coddle his niggers like I did. Oh, they begged me not to sell them to him. They promised that they wouldn't run away but how could I believe them? I sold them, the house, and the land to Jake Pendle and moved down here to New Orleans. I couldn't bear to sell Sampson, however, and he is still with me. Even though he has been free since the War, he refuses to leave my side. It's too bad all the niggers weren't as loyal as my Sampson.

Ruth grew up and was introduced into society. She married well, a banker, who profits when cotton is selling and when it's not. No matter which way the wind blows, bankers always come out ahead. So I've been able to live out my days in comfort with my daughter and grandchildren.

I've often wondered what happened to Emma, Joe, Charles, Winnie, and that little baby of theirs. Did they make it across the Ohio that night? I'm ashamed of myself for thinking this but, from time to time, I've hoped that the boat that carried them across was swamped with water in the storm and went down, drowning them all and whatever nigger-loving white person helped them. But if they lived, if they got the freedom they went seeking, I hope they know that the other slaves paid the price for their freedom.

Interlude X

sampson as an old man

I don't like being old because you have nothing but time to remember. When I look back I don't see much worth remembering. But I remember just the same. The memory I think on the most is that moment when Charles hit me. It wasn't the blows that hurt me. Charles wasn't strong enough to do me any damage with his fists. It was that look on his face that knocked me to the ground and kept me lying there.

I thought I had been a good father to him. He was all I had after his mama died giving birth to him. But that look on his face told me that he despised me. Me! His own father! And if my own son despised me, then I had no choice but to think that my life had been despicable. And that was more than I could bear. I wanted my son to be proud of me, to look up to me as someone he would want to be like. So, I did the only thing I could do.

I didn't tell Mistress Henfield that my Charles and the others had run away, that I had tried to stop them. I knew if I did that she would have sent Jake Pendle after them, and if he caught them, he would've killed them all, including the baby. And I couldn't let that happen.

After Mistress Henfield found out that they was gone, she said they must've set fire to the barn to provide a diversion so they could run away. It never crossed her mind that I might know more than I was saying.

I just wish I didn't have to die and my boy never know that my heart ain't like it was, that I did my part to help him and the others escape. If he knew, he'd be proud of me.

I know he would.

11

On the Road

(Night. The rain comes down in torrents. Joe, Emma, Charles, Winnie, and the baby are hurrying quickly by the side of a road. Their heads are bowed against the stinging rain.)

CHARLES: *(To Joe.)* Do you know where you going? We been walking a long time. What if that white man lied to you? What if this is some kind of trick? Tell me again what Mr. Henry say?

JOE: He say to walk along the big road until we hear an owl hoot three times.

CHARLES: How we gon' hear an owl hoot the way this rain is coming down? We should go back now before Mistress finds out we gone. If we go back now she'll never know what we tried to do.

JOE: What about your papa? He knows. If he ain't told Mistress already, he'll tell her come daybreak. We ain't got no choice. We got to keep going.

CHARLES: I wish I hadn't let you talk me into this.

JOE: Don't you be trying to blame me. Nothing but your own two legs brought you here.

emma

It would be better if Charles would just say he's scared. Instead he gets mad and tries to blame Joe. I'm scared too. We all scared. We're out here cold and wet and tired with no idea of where we're going. Just walking through the darkness 'cause a white man said he knew how we could be free.

I don't want to think about what will happen to us if we don't get free. Mistress will have us whupped until we're as close to death as a person can be and not be dead. Then she'll sell us to Jake

Pendle. I'll kill myself before I let that man be my master.

WINNIE: Emma? What's that?

EMMA: What? I didn't hear nothing.

WINNIE: Up there! Don't you see a light dancing in the darkness?

(Everyone stops and looks.)

CHARLES: I see it! There! We got to get out of here! That's a ghost! Who else would be out on a night like this except a ghost and a bunch of fools like us!

JOE: It might be the patrollers. Quick! We got to hide in the woods! Quick! *(Joe, Emma, Charles, and Winnie, holding her baby tightly to her chest, hurry off the road and into the trees. They watch anxiously as the light comes closer and closer. Joe is the first to recognize that the light is a*

lantern hanging from the side of a wagon, and the hunched figure driving it. He hurries out of the woods and onto the road.)
Mr. Henry! Mr. Henry!

(The wagon stops.)

MR. HENRY: Is that you, Joe?

JOE: Yes, suh. It's me.

MR. HENRY: You must want to be free awful bad to come out on a night like this. I was just about to turn around and go back to town. *(Emma, Charles, and Winnie come out of the woods.)* I see you brought some more travelers.

JOE: Yes, suh.

MR. HENRY: Get in the back. We don't have much time. And you better pray that the folks from Ohio sent somebody across tonight to get you. It wouldn't surprise me if they didn't.

With all this rain, the river could be running too hard to make it across and back safely. And if that's the case, I don't know what we'll do. *(The four climb quickly into the back. Mr. Henry turns the wagon around and heads off rapidly in the direction from which he came.)*

emma

Mr. Henry is driving this wagon like the devil is after him. It bounces around so much it's all we can do not to find ourselves bounced out on the road. We hold on to each other and try and keep our balance.

Nobody says anything but I know we're all thinking it. What if we can't get across tonight? What then? I reckon we could hide out in the woods but by morning Mistress will probably have the dogs after us. And all the white folks will be on the lookout too. We have to get across that river tonight. We have to!

WINNIE: Emma?

EMMA: What's the matter?

WINNIE: My baby . . .

EMMA: What about him?

WINNIE: He's so still.

EMMA: *(Takes the baby from Winnie's arms. She puts her ear to the baby's chest. Tears come into her eyes.)* I-I-I'm sorry, Winnie.

WINNIE: *(Starting to cry.)* No, Emma! No! Not my baby! *(Takes the baby from Emma and begins rocking it in her arms.)* Not my baby!

Interlude XI

jeremiah henry

*I have never driven so hard and so fast in all my life.
More than once I came close to tipping that wagon over,
but God was with me and I will always believe that He
was the one holding the reins that night.*

*If I had been a gambling man I would have wagered
everything in my store that the folks in Ohio would not
have sent anyone across that night. I would have lost that
bet, thank God. When I got to the landing place at the
river I couldn't believe my eyes. The ferry boat was waiting right there. It was raining too hard for me to recognize
the good soul who had brought the boat across, but I hope
God rewarded him with blessings for the rest of his life.*

*I stood there and watched my "passengers" get out of
the wagon. Joe and the tall thin girl gave me big hugs.*

The other boy and the girl with the baby didn't thank me or anything. They had their arms around each other and moved like they were almost dead. All four got on the ferry and I watched until it disappeared in the darkness.

A few days later Mrs. Henfield and Jack Pendle came in the store. I never liked Pendle. He's the kind of man who would kill a slave because whipping would be too much work.

"You wouldn't happen to know anything about four of Mrs. Henfield's slaves escaping, would you?"

My lips said No, but I could feel the look of delight in my eyes and the smile that came over my face as I lied. Well, I knew I wasn't cut out for this kind of work. I don't enjoy lying, not even when the cause is the abolition of slavery. But it was my idea to come south and see what I could do to help some of these poor creatures escape the wretched institution.

But when Mrs. Henfield and Pendle told me that my "passengers" had set the barn on fire and Sampson had almost been killed trying to save the horses and mules, my heart sank. I didn't want to believe them. I was sorry to hear that. Sampson was the kind of slave I didn't have much respect for, though I couldn't fault him. If I'd been a slave, who knows what I would've done? It's entirely possible that I would have found that the best way to survive was to love my master and mistress more than I loved myself.

Even though I'd had nothing to do with Sampson almost being killed, I couldn't escape some responsibility since I was the one who dangled freedom in front of Joe's eyes.

Although Pendle had no proof that I'd been involved in any of the events of that night, that didn't stop him from telling all the plantation owners and townsfolk not to buy at my store. Almost overnight I lost practically all my trade. I knew it was only a matter of time before Pendle would accuse me of aiding runaway slaves and have me arrested. I had no doubt that I would have been convicted.

So one morning I went down to the ferry, got on, and never looked back.

12

Philadelphia

(A year later. Philadelphia. Emma and Joe are walk-
ing along a downtown street on a cloudy day.)

emma

It's different here. Some of the colored people
dress just as good as the white ones. There are
even little stores owned by colored people. And
the white people don't want you to call 'em
"Master" and "Mistress," but "Mister" and
"Missus" or "Miss." They don't use titles when
they speak to us and they call us by our first
names, but there's a little courtesy in their voices
when they do.

Up here everybody has two names. In slavery
we had only one name. I was known as Emma, a
Butler plantation nigger. I suppose if I would

have had a last name it would've been Butler. But I ain't living on the Butler plantation now and I sure ain't nobody's nigger. When me and Joe found out we had to have two names, we talked about it and decided if we were going to be named for anybody it should be Mr. Henry. Without him we would still be living in slavery. It's kind of strange to name yourself after somebody you only knew for a little while, but it ain't how long you know somebody that means anything. It's what that person mean to you in your heart, and Mr. Henry is everything to me and Joe.

Joe and I have our own little house. It's not much, but it's ours even if we have to pay rent for it. I take in laundry from different white people. Joe's working for a blacksmith.

Winnie is here. She's working at a hotel. We see her at church every Sunday. She blame Charles for what happen to the baby and Charles blame Joe for talking him into being free. Winnie don't know where Charles is. He say he can't stay with her no more and he just left.

I feel sorry for them. What happened wasn't nobody's fault. It's like Reverend Collins say in church: the Lord moves in mysterious ways. All we can do is trust in Him.

joe

I wish I liked it here as much as Emma does. She likes the hustle and bustle of the city. I prefer the quiet of the countryside. I miss hearing the birds sing and being able to walk in the woods. I miss seeing things grow. She laughs at me sometimes when I get to talking about wishing I could see cotton out in the field. That don't mean I want to be back in slavery. I don't, but I do miss the beauty that was around me on the Butler plantation.

But I'm not complaining. Life is good here. Me and Emma got married and a real preacher, a colored one, did the wedding in a church! We go to church every Sunday. I sing in the choir and Emma is an usher. She looks so proud every Sunday morning when she puts on her white dress that all the women ushers have to wear. I put on a suit, a white shirt and black tie. Anybody look at us, they wouldn't believe that a year ago we were slaves. I'm taking classes at night to learn how to read and write.

Everything is perfect except that we left so many in slavery. Sometimes I feel guilty that we made it out. If it wasn't for Mr. Henry we wouldn't have. I wish there was a Mr. Henry for all the slaves.

EMMA: *(She stops suddenly and grabs Joe's arm.)* Joe! Look! You see what I see? *(Joe looks in the direction Emma is pointing but doesn't see anything.)* That woman in the long white dress! Up there, Joe! Standing at the corner!

JOE: *(Looks and his eyes get big.)* Have mercy,

Emma! If that ain't Miss Fanny, it's got to be her twin sister! *(Emma runs ahead to the woman standing at the corner.)*

EMMA: Ma'am? Pardon me?

(The woman turns around. She stares for a moment at the girl who is staring up at her with wonderment. Then comes the look of recognition.)

FANNY KEMBLE: Emma? Is that you?

EMMA: It's me, Miss Fanny! It's me!

FANNY KEMBLE: *(Looking at Joe, who has just come up.)* And I recognize your face, but I'm sorry, I don't remember your name.

JOE: That's all right, Miss Fanny. I don't know if you ever knowed it. I'm Joe.

EMMA: He's my husband.

FANNY KEMBLE: Husband! My word! *(Fanny Kemble looks around nervously.)* I don't think it's a good idea for us to be seen talking to each

other on a street corner like we're friends.
Come. Walk with me. *(The three cross the street
and Fanny Kemble leads them down a side street
where there is less traffic and fewer people. Joe and
Emma look at each other, bewildered as to what their
former mistress is doing.)*
    Now. Tell me everything. What are you
doing in Philadelphia? Sarah told me that
you'd been sold away to Kentucky.
EMMA: Yes'm. Me and Joe was sold.

*(Emma tells her the story of their escape. She is
disappointed that Fanny Kemble seems more worried
than elated by their escapade.)*

FANNY KEMBLE: I'm glad you and Joe
were able to get away from slavery, but
you're in danger here in Philadelphia.
JOE: Danger? What do you mean?
FANNY KEMBLE: Pierce Butler has just moved

back to Philadelphia. If he should see you on the street, he could capture you and sell you back into slavery. And don't think he wouldn't do it, because I know he would.

EMMA: Master Butler is here?

FANNY KEMBLE: He's living in a mansion not more than fifteen minutes from here.

(Emma and Joe exchange worried looks.)

JOE: But this is the North. We're free now. How could he sell us back into slavery?

FANNY KEMBLE: There's a new law that says a runaway slave found anywhere in the United States can be captured by any white person who finds him and sold back into slavery.

In fact, that law says I could be arrested for knowing about a runaway and not turning him in to the law.

EMMA: What can we do?

FANNY KEMBLE: I have some friends who can help you escape into Canada.

(The three stop in the shade of a building. They look at each other but the decision has already been made. Joe tells Fanny Kemble where they are living. She promises that someone will come for them that night.)

EMMA: *(As they are preparing to part.)* How's Miss Sarah and Miss Frances?

FANNY KEMBLE: Sarah still talks about you. Thank you for taking such good care of her after I left. Frances? Well, Frances is Frances, but when her father's not around, she'll let on that she misses you, too.

EMMA: I reckon you can't tell them that I miss them, too.

FANNY KEMBLE: I wish I could. But I'm afraid if Pierce found out that I had seen you, he might try to keep me from having what little contact I have with my daughters.

EMMA: I understand. Well, it's good to see you, Miss Fanny.

FANNY KEMBLE: It does my heart good to see you, to know that you're no longer anybody's slave.

(Emma and Fanny Kemble embrace. Then Emma and Joe hurry away just as a gentle rain begins falling.)

Interlude XII

fanny kemble as an old woman

After Pierce died I told Sarah about my meeting Emma on the street. She was upset that I hadn't come and gotten her so she could see Emma, too. But she understood. Those were strange and dangerous times, when unscrupulous white men would kidnap colored men off the streets, men who were free from birth, and sell them into slavery. And the government of the United States did nothing to protect the rights of the colored people, because they had no rights.

While I was overjoyed to see Emma and would've liked nothing better than to take her and Joe into my home, I could not in good conscience put them at risk like that. Immediately after seeing them I got word to someone I knew who was either involved in the business

*of getting runaway slaves into Canada or knew some-
one who did. A few days later I received an unsigned
note that said simply, "The gifts arrived and were sent
safely to their destination."*

*After the War I was visiting Sarah and her family.
One evening she asked me if I knew what had happened
to Emma. I told her I knew only that she and Joe had
reached Canada safely. She wanted to know where in
Canada. I didn't know, but I knew what she was thinking. How could I not, when she had named her first
daughter Emma?*

*I contacted the person who had arranged for Emma
and Joe to go to Canada and learned where they were.
It seems that there are several small towns in Nova
Scotia made up almost entirely of colored people, free-
born Canadians and runaways from slavery. Emma
and Joe had settled in one of them.*

*Sarah wrote and Emma responded. It was very heart-
ening to my Sarah when she learned that Emma had
named her daughter Sarah. And Emma's Sarah read my*

Sarah's letters to her mother and wrote what her mother said in response.

Sarah and Emma longed to see each other again, but travel to Nova Scotia was not easy and Sarah could not have been away from her family for the time such a visit would have required. But Sarah and Emma exchanged photographs, and though both have grandchildren now, they still keep in touch.

I was moved to tears when my Sarah told me what Emma's last words to her had been, that she should have a good heart like her mother's. I never thought of myself as having a good heart, and especially not during that awful time I lived on the Butler plantation. I felt so helpless because there was nothing I could do to make the lives of the slaves better. I wanted to build a school and a hospital for them. I wanted them to own the Butler plantation because they had earned it by their hard labor. But none of that was possible. I left the plantation feeling I had been such a failure.

But perhaps that was because all I could think about

was what I hadn't accomplished. I had not given a thought to what a difference it can make when you treat another person with simple respect and dignity, the same respect and dignity you want for yourself. That is so simple, yet so few seem able to do it.

13

Emma

(Emma stands at a stove in the kitchen. She is an old woman, but she bears a striking resemblance to her mother standing at another stove in another time and another place. The kettle begins to boil and Emma pours water into two cups in which rest straw tea strainers. She sets a cup before a young, dark-skinned woman seated at the table, then takes the other cup to the table and sits down. Outside it is raining lightly.)

EMMA: It was raining the day I gave birth to your mother. Just about like this. A soft, quiet rain. Seems like whenever something important happened in my life it was accompanied by rain. Sometimes it rained hard, so hard that the rain was like needles on your skin. It was strange, but the same rain that helped me and your grandfather to escape from slavery was the same rain that killed Winnie's baby.

After the war what freed the slaves I thought about going back down to Georgia to see if my mama and papa was still alive. But by that time your mama was about your age and she had an older brother and two younger ones and a sister. I didn't have any-one I could leave them with for the months it would have taken me to travel to Georgia and back.

But there's always been a pain in my heart that my mama and papa never knew what happened to me, never knew that I got away from slavery and lived a good life filled with children and grandchildren. *(She pauses and stares into space, her eyes filling with tears. After a moment, she wipes at her eyes and smiles.)*

Here. Let me take that tea strainer out of your cup. I'll put a little milk and sugar in it

and that'll make it cool and sweet for you. I
never had tea until I came here to Nova
Scotia. That's what the folks up here drink. It
took me a while to get used to it, but now I
feel like something's wrong if I don't sit down
in the afternoon and have a cup of tea.

It makes me think about how my mama and
papa would sit in the kitchen on the Butler
plantation and drink coffee. Me and Joe would
drink our tea sitting in our chairs at our table
in our house. He's been dead a long time.
When the War broke out Joe didn't feel right
sitting up here in Canada. He wanted to go
back and be part of the war to free the slaves.
And nothing I said could change his mind.

Didn't nobody have to tell me that he was
dead. One day I woke up and there was a
kind of emptiness inside me. It was a feeling
like I'd never had before and I knew. Joe was
dead. It was a long time before I got a letter. I

took the letter next door to Mrs. Connery and she read it for me. It was from somebody who'd fought alongside Joe and it named the battle he was killed in and said what a brave man he was. I done forgot the name of the battle. The letter is around here somewhere if you want it for that school report you're writing. But I didn't need no letter to tell me that my Joe was dead.

Most days I sit here in the afternoon and it's just me and my tea. Joe used to sit in the chair you're sitting in, and I'll sit here and talk to that chair as if he's still sitting in it. And sometimes he talks back to me.

I know you must think I'm crazy, but it's the truth. I'll hear his voice just as soft and sweet as the rain. *(Again, her eyes gaze into a distance at something, or someone only she sees. Then she turns her attention back to her granddaughter sitting in Joe's chair.)*

You be sure you write in that report of yours that a lot of people, white and black, died because of slavery. I'm thinking about them what died in slavery and them what died to kill slavery. And you be sure and put in there what I told you: all white folks back in that time wasn't evil. If it hadn't been for white people like Mr. Henry, me and Joe wouldn't have made it all the way up here to Nova Scotia. Black and white were conductors on that underground railroad, they called it.

And you be sure and put in that report of yours that I named your mother Sarah for a little white girl who hated slavery, too. She hated wrong and that's because she had a good heart. And that's all that matters in this life. If your heart hurts when you see somebody suffering, you have a good heart.

You understand all that? *(Emma's grand-daughter nods her head.)*

EMMA

I know you do, honey. I know you do.

(Emma's eyes cloud over as her gaze returns to something only she can see. She smiles. The only sound is that of the gentle rain.)

Author's Note

On March 2 and 3, 1859, the largest auction of slaves in American history took place in Savannah, Georgia. Some accounts put the number of slaves sold at 429, while others put it at 436. The slaves were the property of Pierce Butler, the husband of the English actress and abolitionist Fanny Kemble, who is remembered today for her *Journal of a Residence on a Georgian Plantation*.

In 1836 Butler and his brother, John, inherited two plantations in Georgia, one on St. Simon's Island and the other on Butler Island. Over the next twenty years Butler would lose most of his wealth, approximately $700,000, in the stock market and through gambling. In an attempt to satisfy his enormous debts, Butler had to sell his mansion in Philadelphia and other properties. However, this proved insufficient. The only other property Butler owned was slaves, half of the 900 he and his brother had inherited from their grandfather, Major Pierce Butler, a senator from South Carolina, and a signer of the Declaration of Independence, who was also responsible for the fugitive slave clause in the Constitution. Four hundred-fifty slaves, John Butler's half, would remain on the plantation. Pierce's half would be sold.

The 429 or 436 to be sold were placed on railroad cars and steamboats and taken to the Broeck racetrack in Savannah, where they were put in empty horse stalls. On the day of the auction, it started raining, and for the two days of the sale it rained torrentially. However, soon after the auction ended, the rain stopped and the sun came out. The sale became known as "the Weeping Time."

The highest price paid was $6,180 for a woman and her five adult children, while $1,750 was the highest price for one person, and $250 the lowest. Butler gained $303,850.

I am grateful to my editor, Garen Thomas, for bringing "the Weeping Time" to my attention, as it was a story I was not familiar with. I have taken the facts of that story to create a paradigm for the thousands of slave auctions that took place in this country. The only characters taken from the historical account are Pierce Butler and his daughters, Sarah and Frances, the auctioneer, and Fanny Kemble.

The marriage of Pierce Butler and Fanny Kemble ended in divorce for numerous reasons, one being her refusal to be a subservient wife, and another, her opposition to slavery. (When she married him she did not know he owned slaves.) Butler received custody of their two children, each of whom shared the views of slavery held by one of her parents. Sarah was opposed to slavery while Frances defended the institution, and after the Civil War, Frances returned to Butler Island with her father and ran the plantation under the share-cropping system. She subsequently wrote *Ten Years on a Georgia Plantation Since the War*, an apologia for slavery and the "Southern way of life."

This book takes many of the facts from the lives of Pierce Butler and Fanny Kemble and their children but is not a historical recreation of their lives. Rather, history and fiction have been blended. During my research on the slave auction known historically as "the Weeping Time," I happened across a remarkable document, "What became of the slaves on a Georgia plantation?: Great auction sale of slaves, at Savannah, Georgia, March 2d & 3d, 1859. A sequel to Mrs. Kemble's Journal."

This is a pamphlet from the Daniel A. P. Murray Collection housed at the Library of Congress and available over the World Wide Web.

The pamphlet gives a detailed description of the auction and gives the names of some of the slaves and the prices for which they were sold. I have included these in the story without change. Also taken from the pamphlet is the story of Jeffrey and Dorcas as well as the fact that Pierce Butler gave each of his slaves a silver dollar at the end of the auction. The interlude that gives the end to the story of Jeffrey and Dorcas is based on numerous true accounts of the attempts of former slaves to be reunited with loved ones.

History is not only an accounting of what happened when and where. It includes also the emotional biographies of those on whom history imposed itself with a cruelty that we can only dimly imagine. This book is another in my attempts to make real those who did not have the opportunity to tell their stories for themselves.

—Julius Lester

REFERENCES

Fanny Butler Leigh. *Ten Years on a Georgia Plantation Since the War*. Negro Universities Press, 1969.

Catherine Clinton. *Fanny Kemble's Civil Wars*. Simon & Schuster, 2000.

"Fanny Kemble and Pierce Butler."
www.pbs.org/wgbh/aia/part4/4p1569.html

"The Weeping Time."
www.pbs.org/wgbh/aia/part4/4p2918.html

"The Largest Slave Auction."
America's Story from America's Library.
www.americaslibrary.gov/cgi-bin/page.cgi/jb/reform/slaveauc_1

African American Perspectives: Pamphlets from the Daniel A. P. Murray Collection, 1818–1907. "What became of the slaves on a Georgia plantation?: Great auction, of slaves, at Savannah, Georgia, March 2d & 3d, 1859. A sequel to Mrs. Kemble's Journal." Library of Congress, Rare Book and Special Collections Division.
hdl.loc.gov/loc.rbc/lcrbmrp.t2305

Q&A with Julius Lester

Q. What was the inspiration for this novel?
A. I know people think writers get "inspired," but the reality is sometimes different. The idea for the novel came from Garen Thomas, my editor at Hyperion. I was unfamiliar with what history calls "The Weeping Time." I found the idea intriguing, and did some research to see what the story possibilities were. The fact that the auction was done for the benefit of Pierce Butler was further intriguing, as he was married to Fanny Kemble, a remarkable woman whose name I was familiar with. I read several biographies of Fanny Kemble, as well as the book her youngest daughter wrote defending slavery. If there was a moment of "inspiration" it came when I saw a notice for a photo show in a magazine. (I am also a photographer.) The photo was a 19th-century daguerreotype of a nine- to ten-year-old slave girl holding a white girl of about two or three on her lap. I kept that photo on my desk as I wrote the book.

Q. Day of Tears *is a mixture of history and fiction. How did you craft your story around the historical facts?*
A. I've written a lot of historical fiction set during slavery. So, the facts of what life was like during slavery are things I know from past research, and I don't have to research anew. The key to historical fiction is making the characters believable and real, and this means integrating the facts into the narrative so they aren't even recognizable as facts. But the other side of historical fiction is ignoring the history to make a better story. For example, *Day of Tears* opens on the last day of the slave auction, and there is the scene in which slaves are taken to the barn and put into a wagon and taken into town. Historically, all the slaves were moved to town before the first day of the auction. Dramatically, however, it was better to have a scene in which the slaves are being moved.

Q. How did you choose the format for this novel? Do you see it as a future play?
A. I don't see this as a play. I don't like plays. I think I came to the format because, as I said, I've written a lot of historical fiction based on slavery, and I didn't want to repeat myself. So, I wondered, how could I approach this story in a different way? Not sure how the idea of doing it in dialogue came to me, but when it did, I was intrigued by the challenge. Could I convey a sense of place and character without descriptive sections?

I had a call-in radio show in New York from 1968 to 1975. I loved radio, because all you had to use was your voice. So, in writing the novel I think I drew on my years in radio and my consciousness of how much the voice can convey.

Q. What do you hope readers will take from this novel?
A. I never know how to answer this question. I have also written adult fiction, and this is not a question I get asked about my adult books. There seems to be an assumption that children's books have a didactic element. I just hope the readers are moved by the various stories in the novel.

Q. How did you become interested in writing books for young people?
A. I write for all ages. I've done picture books, YA novels, nonfiction, poetry, and fiction and nonfiction for adult readers. I wonder sometimes if the way we categorize books isn't artificial, more something that is market-driven than [something that] has any reality in the writing of the books. I like to tell stories, and there is more opportunity to do that in books for children, as well as science fiction and fantasy. I simply see myself as a writer, and adults read my YA books and never know that [they were] marketed for YA. I just write, and the books find the readers they're supposed to have.